BROWNIES
& BOGLES

A Compendium of Enchanting
Fairy Lore

ABOUT THE AUTHOR

LOUISE IMOGEN GUINEY (1861–1920) was an American poet, essayist, and editor, celebrated for her evocative verses and insightful prose. Born in Massachusetts, Guiney's literary talents blossomed early, leading to her association with the Boston literary scene of the late 19th century. Guiney's writing often explored spirituality, nature, and the human condition, reflecting her intellectual curiosity.

foreword by Chris Allaun, author of *Whispers from the Coven*

Louise Imogen Guiney

BROWNIES & BOGLES

A Compendium of Enchanting Fairy Lore

CROSSED CROW BOOKS
TEXTS OF ANTIQUITY

Chicago, Illinois

Originally published in 1888 by D. Lothrop Company.

Illustrated by Edmund H. Garrett.

Paperback ISBN: 978-1-964537-01-6
Library of Congress Control Number on file.

Published by:
Crossed Crow Books, LLC
6934 N Glenwood Ave, Suite C
Chicago, IL 60626
www.crossedcrowbooks.com

Printed in the United States of America.
IBI

 # CONTENTS

FOREWORD

I was raised in rural Texas. We lived so far into the country that it was a thirty-minute drive to the nearest small town. I didn't appreciate it when I was a kid, but growing up I had more in common with Laura Ingles and Huckleberry Finn than I wanted to admit. Where I grew up, there were cow pastures, horse ranches, farms, open prairies, and lots of wooded areas. We didn't own a farm ourselves, but we had lots of animals and the land to us was sacred.

Behind our property was a wooded area that the kids knew to be haunted. Haunted by what, well, that depends on the story that was being told that day. Some of the ol' timers would say it was haunted by the dead animals that were dragged there to rot. You see, burying a horse or a cow was no easy task, so sometimes they would drag the carcass in the woods for the coyotes to feast on. Other people would say there were strange spirits who lived "in between" the trees.

My brothers, our friends, and I spent a lot of time in those haunted woods. To me, the trees had a voice of their own. When I was little, I didn't understand it too much, but we knew those trees had a kind of power. An otherworldly power. We knew to never ever be in those woods after sundown. No one had to tell us, it was a feeling we had in our bones. During the day, those old woods were "safe," but come nightfall, well…let's just say we weren't stupid enough to find out what came out in the dark.

One time, my brothers and I were following this little stream that was formed because of the Texas rains. It wasn't deep at all, but deep enough to make a tiny river going through those woods. We were following the little river and off in the distance was a creature we'd never seen before. It had big eyes, tan fur, and what looked to be wings. It stood about three feet tall and took notice of us. It saw us and we saw it. Before we could even speak, it vanished. That was the first time I saw a nature spirit "in the flesh." When I mean "flesh," I mean it wasn't a reflection of light, our imaginations, or even a spirit. It was flesh and blood. It seemed to be able to read our thoughts and, for a minute, we could read its thoughts. We weren't supposed to see it and it knew it! That was the first time I saw a "fairy" creature in those woods.

In my tradition of witchcraft and paganism, faeries, elves, and other nature spirits play a big role in our cosmology. As humans, we are "of the land," and so we are taught that these spirits are kindred to us. Not the same as us, but we share a connection to the land, the sea, and the skies. The earth is our home, and the faeries, elves, and nature spirits share our home with us. In my circle, we honor these beings with offerings and love.

I'm a lover of paganism, myth, history, and storytelling, so I was delighted to be asked to write the foreword to this book. I've read many books from the nineteenth century on magic, myth, and folklore, and this book fits right in with many of the pagan classics that were written in this time period. The author, Louise Imogen Guiney, wrote this book in such a way that I could see that she took great delight in researching the folklore of the fairies, elves, brownies, and many other "fairy" beings.

As you read this book, keep in mind that it was written in the Victorian era and has some "sensibilities" from that time period. What I mean by this is that during that time fairies are thought to be little winged sprites, water spirits are dangerous, and the word "fairy" is a generic term for many Otherworldly beings. For me, these descriptions helped take me back to the time it was written…1888. I like to think the protagonist in my Witch story book, Jonathan Knotbristle, most likely had this book and even used it as a resource and guide to the nature spirits of the Otherworld. I can see him now in his rocking chair, smoking his pipe and drinking whiskey as he flipped through the pages of this book. Jonathan Knotbristle probably knew some of these fairies by name! He was the type of witch who was friend to human and fairy alike. He paid no mind to what was what.

What intrigued me the most about this book, as a storyteller, is the care and research that Louise Imogen Guiney did as she was collecting these stories. You see, in these pages are the legends and folktales of the spirits who lived not only in the Otherworld, but also in the trees, the waters, and even in our own homes. Oh, yes, there are spirits who will live in our homes and they will…well, I'll let Louise tell you the rest. She has a knack for storytelling.

Well, dear reader, pour yourself a cup of tea, sit back in your chair, and allow yourself to be astrally transported back to the late nineteenth century, where everyone in town knew the tales of the fairies. Careful now, no matter what the townsfolk say, be respectful. Say only good things about the fairies, give them a cup of cream, or pour them some whiskey. Better to make a fairy your friend then…well. Turn the page and you will see.

—Chris Allaun, author of *The Black Book of Johnathan Knotbristle* and *Whispers from the Coven*

CHAPTER ONE

WHAT FAIRIES WERE AND WHAT THEY DID

A fairy is a humorous person sadly out of fashion at present, who has nevertheless had, in the actors' phrase, a long and prosperous run on this planet. When we speak of fairies nowadays, we think only of small sprites who live in a kingdom of their own, with manners, laws, and privileges very different from ours. But there was a time when "fairy" suggested also the knights and ladies of romance, about whom fine spirited tales were told when the world was younger. Edmund Spenser's "The Faerie Queene," for instance, deals with dream-people, beautiful and brave, as do the old stories of Arthur and Roland: people who either never lived, or who, having lived, were glorified and magnified by tradition out of all kinship with common people.

Our fairies are fairies in the modern sense. We will make it a rule, from the beginning, that they must be small, and we will put out any who are above the regulation height. For example, the charming and famous Melusina, who wails upon her tower at the death of a Lusignan, we may as well skip for she is a tall young lady, with a serpent's tail to boot, and thus (alas!), she is

1

half-monster; if we should accept any like her in our plan, there is no reason why we should not get confused among mermaids and dryads, and perhaps end by scoring down great Juno herself as a fairy. Many a dwarf and goblin, whom we shall meet, are as big as a child. Yet, there are rumors in nearly every country of finding hundreds of them on a square inch of oak-leaf, or beneath the thin shadow of a blade of grass. The fairies of popular belief are little and somewhat shriveled, and quite as apt to be malignant as to be frolicsome and gentle. We shall find that they were divided into several classes and families, but there is much analogy and vagueness among these divisions. By and by, you may care to study them for yourselves; at present, we shall be very high-handed with the science of folklore and pay no attention whatsoever to the learned, who quarrel so foolishly about these things that it is not helpful—nor even funny—to listen to them. A widely spread notion is that when crusading Christians went to the Holy Land, they heard the Muslim soldiers, whom they fought, speaking much of the Peri: the loveliest beings imaginable, who dwelt in the East. Now, the Arabic language, which these warriors used, has no letter P, and therefore they called their spirits *Feri*, as did the Crusaders after them; the word went back with them to Europe and slipped into general use.

"Elf" and "goblin," too, are interesting to trace. There was a great Italian feud in the twelfth century between the German Emperor and the Pope, whose separate partisans were known as the Guelfs and the Ghibellines. As time went on, with the memory of that long strife still fresh, a descendant of the Guelfs would put the odious name of *Ghibelline* upon anybody they disliked; the latter, generation after generation, would return the compliment ardently in their own fashion. Both terms, finally, came to be mere words for abuse and reproach. The fairies, falling into disfavor with some bold mortals, were angrily nicknamed "elf" and "goblin," in which shape you will recognize the last threadbare reminder of the once bitter and historic factions of Guelf and Ghibelline.

It is likely that the tribe was designated as fairies because they were, for the most part, fair to see and full of grace and charm, especially among the Celtic branches. People, at all times, have too much desire to keep their goodwill, and too much shrinking from their rancor and spite to give them any but the most flattering titles. They were seldom addressed in ways other than "the little folk," "the kind folk," "the gentry," "the fair family," "the blessings of their mothers," and "the dear wives," just as, thousands of years back, the noblest and cleverest nation the world has ever seen called the dreaded Three Eumenides "the gracious ones." It is a sure and fast maxim that wheedling human nature puts on its best manners when it is afraid. In Oliver Goldsmith's racy play *She Stoops to Conquer,* old Mistress Hardcastle meets what she takes to be a robber. She hates robbers, of course, and is scared half out of her five wits, but she implores mercy, with a cowering politeness at which nobody can choose but laugh, of her "good Mr. Highwayman."[1] Now, fairies, who knew how to be bountiful and tender and who made slaves of themselves to serve humans, as we shall see, were easily offended and wrought great mischief and revenge if they were not treated handsomely, all of which kept people in the habit of courtesy toward them. A whirlwind of dust is a very annoying thing, making one splutter and feel absurdly

---

1   Goldsmith, Oliver, *She Stoops to Conquer* (1773)

resentful, but in Ireland and modern Greece, it was thought that it betokened the presence of fairies going a journey, so they lifted their hats gallantly and said: "Godspeed you, gentlemen!"

"Godspeed you, Gentlemen!"

Fairies had their followers and votaries from early times. Nothing in the Bible hints that they were known among the heathens with whom the Israelites warred; nothing in classic mythology has any approach to them, except the beautiful wood and water nymphs. Yet the poet Homer, Pliny the scientist, and Aristotle the philosopher had some notion of them and their influence. In ancient China, whole mountains were peopled with them, and the coriander seeds grown in their gardens gave long life to those who ate them. The Persians had a hierarchy of elves and were the first to set aside Fairyland as their dwelling-place. Saxons, in their wild forests, believed in tiny dwarves or demons called *Duergar.* Celtic countries, like Scotland, Brittany, Ireland, and Wales, were always crowded with them. In the uttermost mountains of India, under a merry part of heaven or by the hoary Nile (according to other writers), were the Pigmeos: one cubit (eighteen inches) high, full-grown at three years and old at seven, who fought with cranes for a livelihood. And the Swiss alchemist Paracelsus (a most pompous and amusing old bigwig) wrote that in his day, all of Germany was filled with fairies two feet long, walking about in little coats!

The fairies' favorite color, especially in Great Britain, was green; the majority of them wore it and grudged its adoption by a mortal. Sir Walter Scott tells us that it was a fatal hue to several families in his country; it was so to the entire gallant race of Grahames in particular, for in battle, a Grahame was almost always shot through the green check of his plaid.[2] French fairies went in white; the Nis of Jutland, and many other house-sprites, in red and gray or red and brown; and the plump Welsh goblins, whose holiday dress was also white, in the brightest and most varied tints of all. In North Wales were "the old elves of the blue petticoat"; in Cardiganshire was the familiar green again, though it was never seen save in the month of May; and in Pembrokeshire,

---

2   Scott, Walter, "Notes on Canto Fourth" in *Lady of the Lake* (1810)
     p. 388

a uniform of jolly scarlet gowns and caps. The fairy gentlemen were quite given to finery as much as the ladies, and their general air was one of extreme cheerful dandyism. Only the mine and ground-fairies were attired in somber colors. Indeed, their idea of clothes was delightfully liberal; an elf bespoke themselves by what they chose to wear, and fashions ranged all the way from the sprites of the Orkney Islands, who strutted about in armor, to the little Heinzelmänchen of Cologne, who scorned to be burdened with so much as a hat!

People accounted in strange ways for their origin. A legend firmly held in Iceland says that once upon a time, Eve was washing a number of her children at a spring, and when the Lord appeared suddenly before her, she hustled and hid away those who were not already clean and presentable; they, being made forever invisible after, became the ancestors of the "little folk," who pervade the hills and caves and ruins to this day. In Ireland and Scotland, fairies were spoken of as a wandering remnant of the fallen angels. The Christian world over, they were deemed to be locked out from the happiness of the blessed in the next world, either for a while or perpetually. The Bretons thought their Korrigans had been great Gallic princesses who refused the new faith, clung to their Pagan gods, and fell under a curse because of their stubbornness. The Small People of Cornwall, too, were imagined to be the ancient inhabitants of that country long before Christ was born, not good enough for Heaven and yet too good to be condemned altogether, whose fate it is to stray about, growing smaller and smaller, until they vanish from the face of the earth.

Therefore, the poor fairy-folk, with whom theology deals so rudely, were supposed to be tired, waiting, and anxious to know how they might fare everlastingly; they waylaid many mortals—who, of course, really could tell them nothing—to ask whether they might not get into Heaven, by chance, at the end. It was their chief cause of doubt and melancholy, and ran in their little minds from year to year. And since we shall revert no more to the sad side of fairy-life, let us close with a most sweet story of something which happened in Sweden centuries ago.

Two boys were gambolling by a river when a Neck rose up to the air, smiling and twanging his harp. The elder child watched him and cried mockingly: "Neck! What is the good of your sitting there and playing? You will never be saved!" The Neck's sensitive eyes filled with tears and, dropping his harp, he sank forlornly to the bottom. But when the brothers had gone home and told their wise and saintly father, he said they had been thoughtlessly unkind; he bade them hurry back to the river and comfort the little water-spirit. From far off, they saw him again on the surface, weeping bitterly. And they called to him: "Dear Neck! Do not grieve, for our father says that your Redeemer liveth also." Then he threw back his bright head, and, taking his harp, sang and played with exceeding gladness until sunset was long past and the first star sent down its benediction from the sky.

CHAPTER TWO

FAIRY RULERS

T he forming of character among the fairy-folk was a very simple and sensible matter. You will imagine that the Pagan, Druid, and Christian elves varied greatly. And they did; still, their morals had nothing to do with it, nor pride, patriotism, descent, nor education, nor would all the philosophy you might crowd into a thimble have made one bee-big resident of Japan different from one of their own size in Spain.

The fairy-folk saved themselves no end of trouble by setting up the local barometer as their standard. The only Bible they knew was the weather, and they followed it stoutly. Whatever the climate was—whatever it had helped to make the grown-up nation who lived under it—that, every time, were the brownies and bogles. Where the land was rocky and grim, subject to wild storms and sudden darknesses, the fairies were grim and wild too, and full of wicked tricks. Where the landscape was level and green and the crops grew peacefully, they were tame and inclined to be sentimental (as in central England).

They copied the distinguishing traits of the groups among whom they dwelt. A frugal Breton fairy spoke the Breton dialect; the Neapolitan had a tooth for fruits and macaroni; the Chinese was ceremonious and stern; a true Provençal fée was as vain as a peacock, flirting a mirror before her; and an Irish elf (bless his little red-feathered caubeen!) was never the man to run away from a fight.

If you look on the map and see a section of coastline like that of Cornwall or Norway, a sunshiny, perilous, foamy place, make up your mind that the fairies thereabouts were fellows worth knowing. You would have needed all your wit and pluck to get the better of them, and they would have made live, hearty playmates, too, while in good humor, for any brave soul.

We do not know nearly so much about the genuine fairies as we should like. They must have been, at one time or another, in every European country. Most of the Asian spirits were taller and of another brood; they figured either as demons, or as what we should now call angels. But in the Germanic colonies, from very old days, fairy-lore was finely developed, and we count up tribe on tribe of necks, nixies, *stromkarls,* and mermaids, who were water-sprites; of *bergmännchen* (little men of the mountain) and lovely wild-women in hilly places; of trolls around the woods and rocks; of elves in the air and gnomes or *duergars* in caverns or mines. Yet from Portugal, Russia, Hungary, and from our own Native Americans, we learn so little that it is not worth counting.

If the good dear peasants who were acquainted with the fairies had made more rhymes about them, and handed them down more attentively, if it had occurred to the knowing scholar-monks to keep diaries of elfin doings, as it would have been done had they but known how soon their little friends were to be extinct like the glyptodon and the dodo, how wise should we now be!

The Neapolitan Fairy

But again, though there were hosts of supernatural beings in the beliefs of every old land, we have no business with any but the wee ones. And as these were settled most thickly in the Teutonic, Celtic, and Cymric countries, we will turn our curiosity thither without farther grumbling and be glad to get so much authentic news of them as we may.

Fairies, as a whole, seem at bottom rather weak and disconsolate. For all of their magic and cunning, for all of their high station and its feasting and glory, they could not keep from seeking human sympathy. They did, indeed, hurt humans, resent intrusions, foretell the future, and call down disease and storm, but they stood in awe of the weakest mortal because of their superior strength and size; fairies came to them to borrow food and medicine, and even to ask the loan of a human's house for their revels. They rendered themselves invisible, but always had at their feet the fern-seed, the talisman of four-leaved clover (or, as in Scotland, the leaf of the ash or rowan tree), with which they could defeat their design and protect themselves against the attacks of any witch, imp, or fairy whatsoever.

Their government was a happy-go-lucky affair. The various tribes of fairies had no common interests which would make them sigh for post offices, cables, or general synods. Each set of them got along, independent of the rest. Once in a while, a mine-man would live alone with his wife, toiling away at his daily work, without any idea of hurrahing for his King or, more likely, his Queen, or even of hunting up his own cousins in the next county.

If we had elves in the United States nowadays, they would no doubt be American enough to elect a President and have them as honest, and steady, and sound-hearted as needs be. But dwelling as they did in feudal days, they set up thrones and scepters all over Fairydom.

According to many poets, Mab and Oberon are the crowned rulers of the Fairy People. In reality, they had no supreme head. Among many parties and factions, each small agreeing community had its own chief, the tallest of his race, who was no chief at all, mind you, to the fairy neighbors a mile east. The delicate Chinese fairy-mother was Si Wang Mu, and in the Netherlands, the elf-queen, who was also queen of the witches, was called Wanne Thekla.

We snatch an item here and there of the royal histories. We find that the sweet-natured Elberich in the Niebelungen is the same as Oberon. In Germany was a dwarf-king named Goldemar, who lived with a knight, shared his bed, played at dice with him, gave him good advice, called him Brother-in-law very fondly, and comforted him with the music of his harp. But Goldemar, though the knight loved him and could touch and feel him, was unseen. He was like a wreath of blue smoke, or a fragment of moonlight, and you could run a sword through him and never change his kind smile. His royal hands were lean, soft, and cold as a frog's. After three years, perhaps when Brother-in-law was dead or married and needed him no longer, the gentle dwarf-king disappeared.

Sinnels, Gübich, and Heiling were other dwarf-princes, probably rivals of Goldemar, and ready to have at him till their breath gave out. Their little majesties were quarrelsome as sparrows. The elf-monarch Laurîn was once conquered by Theodoric, and because he had been treacherous in war (which was not "fair" at all, despite the proverb), he got a very sad rebuff to his dignity, made fool or buffoon at the court of Bern.

The elf-monarch who was made court-fool

We are told in the *Mabinogion* how the daughter of Llud Llaw Ereint was "the most splendid maiden in the three islands of the mighty," and how for her, Gwyn ap Nudd, the Welsh fairy-king, battles every May Day from dawn until sunset. Gwyn once carried her off from Gwythyr, her true lord, and both lovers were so furious and cruel against each other that blessed King Arthur condemned them to wage bitter fights on each first of May until the world's end, and to whomsoever is victorious the greatest number of times, the fair lady shall then be given. Let us hope the reward will not fall to thieving Gwyn.

We have said that we should do pretty much as we pleased in ranging the myriad fairy-folk into ranks and species. If, as we prowl about, we see a baby in the house of the Elfsmiths, who has a look of the Elfbrowns, we will immediately kidnap them from their fond parents and add them to the family they resemble. Now that might make wailing and confusion and bring down vengeance on our heads if there were any Queen Mab left to rap us to order, but as things go, we shall find it a very neat way of smoothing difficulties.

Of course there are certain pigwidgeons too accomplished, too slippery, too many things in one to be ticketed and tied down like the rest—such versatile fellows as the Brown Dwarves of the Isle of Rügen, for instance. They lived in what were called the Vine-hills and were not quite eighteen inches high. They wore little snuff-brown jackets and a brown cap (which made them invisible and allowed them to pass through the smallest keyhole) with one wee silver bell at its peak, not to be lost for any money. But they did some roguish things, and children who fell into their hands had to serve them for fifty years! With caprice usual to their kin, they will, on other occasions, befriend and protect children and give them presents, or plague untidy servants, like Brownie, or lead travellers astray by night into bogs and marshes, like the Ellydan, the Fir-Darrig, and mischievous double-faced Robin Goodfellow himself.

An ancient tradition says that while the grass-blades are sprouting at the root, the earth-elves water and nourish them; the moment the growth pierces the soil, affectionate air-elves take it in charge. Therefore, we borrow a hint from the grass, and after first going down among the swarthy fairies who burrow underground, we shall pass up to companionship with little beings so beautiful that wherever they flock there is starlight and song.

The Isle of Rügen dwarves that give presents to children

CHAPTER THREE

THE DARK ELVES

According to the very old Scandinavian notion, land-fairies were of two sorts: the Light or Good Elves who dwelt in air or out-of-doors on the earth, and the Dark or Evil Elves who dwelt beneath it.

We will follow the Norse folk. If we were required to group human beings under two headings, we should choose that same good and evil—because the division occurs to one naturally, it saves time, and everybody comprehends it—and so do we deal with our wonder-friends, who have the strange moral sorcery belonging to each of us their masters, to help or to harm.

The evil fairies, then, were the scowling underground tribes, who hid themselves from the frank daylight and the open reaches of the fields. Yet, just as the good fairies had many a sad failing to offset their grace and charm, the grim, dark-skinned manikins had sudden impulses towards honor and kindness. In fact, as we noted before, they were astonishingly like our fellow creatures, of whom scarcely any are entirely faultless or entirely warped and ruined.

The dwarf that borrowed the silk gown

For instance, the Hill-men in Switzerland were very generous-minded; they drove home stray lambs at night and put berry-bushes in the way of poor children. And the more modern dwarves of Germany, frequenting the clefts of rocks, were silent, mild, and well-disposed, and apt to bring presents to those who took their fancy. Like others of the elf-kingdom, they loved to borrow from mortals. Once a little bowing dwarf came to a lady for the loan of her silk gown for a fairy-bride. (You can imagine that, at the ceremony, the groom must have had a pretty hunt among the wilderness of finery to get at her ring finger!) Of course the lady gave it, but worrying over its tardy return, she went to the dwarves' hill and asked for it aloud. A messenger with a sorrowful countenance brought it to her at once, spotted over and over with wax. But he told her that had, she been less impatient, every stain would have been a diamond!

The huge, terrible, ogre-like Hindu Rakshas, the Divs and Jinns of Persia, and the ancient demon-dwarves of the south called Panis, may be considered the foster-parents of our dwindled minims, as the glorious Peris on the other hand gave their name, and some of their qualities, to a little European family of very different ancestry.

The Dark Elves will serve as our general name for dwarves and mine-fairies. These are closely connected in all legends, living in the same neighborhoods, and therefore claim a mention together. They have four points in common: dark skin; short, bulky bodies; fickle and irritable natures; and occupations as miners, misers, or metalsmiths. And because of their exceeding industry on the old maxim's authority, where all work and no play made Jack a dull boy, they are curiously heavy-headed and preposterous jacks and, waiving their plain faces, not in any ways engaging. Yet perhaps, being largely German, they may be philosophers, and so vastly superior to any little gabbling, somersaulting ragamuffin over in Ireland.

In the Middle Ages, they were described as withered and leering, with small, sharp, snapping black eyes, bright as gems, with cracked voices, matted hair, and horns peering from it! And as if that were not enough adornment, they had claws (which must have been filched from the ghosts of mediæval cats) on their fingers and toes.

The first Duergars, belonging to the Gotho-German mythology, were muscular and strong-legged; when they stood erect, their arms reached to the ground. They were clever and expert handlers of metal and made the finest armor in the world of gold, silver, and iron. They wrought for Odin his great spear, and for Thor his hammer, and for Frey the wondrous ship *Skidbladnir*.

Long ago, too, armor-making Elves, dark as pitch, lived in Svart-Alfheim, in the bowels of the earth, and were able, by their glance or touch or breath, to cause sickness and death wheresoever they wished.

Still uglier were the Dark Dwarves of the mysterious Isle of Rügen; nor had they any frolicsome or cordial ways which should bring up our opinion of them. Their pale eyes ran water, and every midnight they mewed and screeched horribly from their holes. In idle summer hours they sat under the elder trees, planning by twos and threes to wreak mischief on humankind. They, as well, were once useful, if not beautiful; for in the days when heroes wore a panoply of steel, the Dark Dwarves wrought fair helmets and corselets of cobwebby mail which no lance could pierce, and swords flexible as silk which could unhorse the mightiest foe. The little dwarves frequented mining districts and dug for ore on their own account. They were said to be very rich, owning unnumbered chests stored underground. The most exciting tales about gnomes of all nations were founded on the efforts of daring mortals to get possession of their wealth.

To the mining division belong the dwarf-Trolls of Denmark and Sweden (for there were giant-Trolls as well), and the whimsical Spriggans of Cornwall. The Trolls burrowed in mounds and hills and were called also Bjerg-folk or Hill-folk; they lived in societies or families, baking and brewing, marrying and visiting, in the old humdrum way. They made fortunes and hoarded heaps of money. But they were often obliging and benevolent; it gave them pleasure to bestow gifts, to lend and borrow, and sometimes (alas!) to steal. They played prettily on musical instruments and were very jolly. People used to see the stumpy little children of the genteel Troll who lived at Kund in Jutland, climbing up the knoll which was the roof of their own house, and rolling down one after the other with shouts of laughter. The Trolls were famous gymnasts, and very plump and round. Our word "droll" is left to us in merry remembrance of them.

Trolls were tractable creatures, as you may know from the tale of the farmer, who, ploughing an angry Troll's land, agreed for the sake of peace to go halves in the crops sown upon it, so that one year the Troll should have what grew above ground and the next year what grew under. But the sly farmer planted radishes and carrots, and the Troll took the tops; the following season he planted corn and his odd little partner gathered up the roots and marched off in triumph. Indeed, it was so easy to outwit the simple Troll that a generous farmer would never have played the game out, and we should have lost our little story. It was mean to take advantage of the sweet fellow's trustfulness. There was an English schoolmaster once—a man wise, firm, and kind, and of vast influence—of whom one of his boys said to another: "It's a shame to tell a lie to Arnold; he always believes it." That was a ray of real chivalry.

The Troll's Children

The Spriggans were fond of dwelling near walls and loose stones, with which it was unlucky to tamper, and where they slipped in and out with suspicious eyes, guarding their buried treasure. If a house was robbed, or the cattle were carried away, or a hurricane swooped down on a Cornish village, the neighbors attributed their trouble to the Spriggans, whereby you may believe they had fine reputations for meddlesomeness. Their cousins, the Buccas, Bockles, or Knockers, were gentlemen who went about thumping and rapping wherever there was a vein of ore for the weary workmen, cheating, occasionally, to break the monotony.

The Welsh Coblynau followed the same profession and pointed out the desirable places in mines and quarries. The Coblynau were copper-colored and very homely, as were all those who lived away from the sun; they were busybodies, half-a-yard high, who imitated the dress of their friends the miners and pegged away at the rocks like them with great noise and gusto, accomplishing nothing. Their houses were far-removed from mortal vision, and unlike certain proper children now obsolete, the Coblynau themselves were generally heard but not seen.

A Coblynau

Their German relation was the *Wichtlein* (little wight), an extremely small fellow, whom the Bohemians named *Hans-schmiedlein* (little John Smith!) because he makes a noise like the stroke of an anvil.

Dwarves and mine-men went about, unfailingly, with a purse full of gold. But if anyone snatched it from them, only stones and twine and a pair of scissors were to be found in it. The Leprechaun, or *Cluricaune,* whom we shall meet later as the fairy-cobbler, was an Irish celebrity who knew where pots of gold coins were hidden, and who carried in his pocket a shilling often-spent and ever-renewed. He looked, in this banker-like capacity, a clumsy small boy, dressed in various ways, sometimes in a long coat and cocked hat, unlike the Danish Troll, who kept to homely gray with the universal little red cap. Even the respectable Kobold, who was virtually a house-spirit, caught the fever of fortune-hunting and often threw up his domestic duties to seek the fascinating nuggets in the mines.

There is a funny anecdote of a Troll who, as was common with his race, cunningly concealed his prize under the shape of a coal. Now a peasant on his way to church one bright Sunday morning saw him trying vainly to move a couple of crossed straws which had blown upon his coal, for anything in the shape of a cross seemed to shrivel up an elf's power in the most startling manner. So the little sprite turned, half-crying, and begged the peasant to move the straws for him. But the man was too shrewd for that. He took up the coal, straws and all, and ran, despite the poor Troll's screaming. On reaching home, he saw that he had captured a lump of solid gold.

All Dark Elves were particular about their neighborhoods, and a whole colony would migrate at once if they took the least offence, or if the villagers about got "too knowing" for them. (An American poet once wrote a sonnet "To Science," in which he berated her for having made him "too knowing," and for having driven "the Naiad from her flood / The elfin from the green grass" and it was in consequence of his very knowingness, no doubt, that beauty-loving and marvel-loving as were his sensitive eyes, they never saw so much as the vanishing shadow of a fairy.)[3] A little dwarf-woman told two young Bavarians that she intended to leave her favorite dwelling, because of the shocking cursing and swearing of the country-people! But they were not all so godly.

"I can't stay any longer!"

---

3   Poe, Edgar Allen, "Sonnet—To Science" in *Al Aaraaf, Tamerlane, and Minor Poems* (Hatch and Dunning, 1829)

CHAPTER FOUR

THE LIGHT ELVES

Over the beautiful Light Elves of the *Edda*, in old Scandinavia, ruled the beloved sun god Frey. They lived in a summer land called Alfheim, and it was their office to sport in air or on the leaves of trees, and to make the earth thrive.

But they changed character as centuries passed, and they came to resemble the fairies of Great Britain in their extreme waywardness and fickleness. Though they were fair and benevolent most of the time, they could be, when it so pleased them, ugly and hurtful, and what they could be, they very often were, for fairies were not expected to keep a firm rein on their moods and tempers.

Norwegian peasants described some of their *Huldrafolk* as tiny bare boys with tall hats; and in Sweden, as well, they were slender and delicate. When a Swedish elf-maid or moon-maid wished to approach the inmates of a house, she rode on a sunbeam through the keyhole, or between the openings in a shutter.

The German wild-women were like them, having fine hair flowing to their feet and going about alone. They had some odd

An elle-maid of Denmark

traits, one of which was sermonizing and exhorting stray mortals who had done them a service to lead a godly life.

The elle-maid in Denmark and neighboring countries was always winsome and graceful, and carried an enchanted harp. She loved moonlight best and was a charming dancer. But her evil element was in her very beauty, with which she entrapped foolish young gentlemen, waylaid them, and carried them off who knows whither. She could be detected by the shape of her back, being hollow like a spoon, which was meant to show that there was something wrong with her, and that she was not what she seemed but fit only for the abhorrence of passers-by. The elle-man, her mate, was old and ill-favored, a disagreeable person, for if anyone came near him while he was bathing in the sun, he opened his mouth and breathed pestilence upon them.

A common trait of the air-fairies was to assist at a birth and give the infant, at their will, good and bad gifts. Dame Bertha, the White Lady of Germany, came to the birth of certain princely babes, and the Korrigans made it a general practice. Whenever they nursed or tended to a newborn mortal, bestowed presents on them and foretold their destiny; one of the attendees was almost always perverse enough to bestow and foretell something unfortunate. You all know Grimm's beautiful tale of *Dornröschen*, which in English we call "The Sleeping Beauty," where the jealous thirteenth fairy predicts the poor young lady's spindle-wound. Around the famous Roche des Fées in the forest of Theil are those who believe that the elves pass in and out at the chimneys on errands to little children.

Bertha, the White Lady

The modern Greek fairies haunted trees, danced rounds, bathed in cool water, and carried off whomsoever they coveted. A person offending them in their own fields was smitten with disease.

The Chinese Shan Sao were a foot high, lived among the mountains, and were afraid of nothing. They, too, were revengeful, for if they were attacked or annoyed by mortals, they caused them to sicken with alternate heat and cold. Bonfires were burnt to drive them away.

The innocent White Dwarves of the Isle of Rügen in the Baltic Sea made lacework of silver, too fine for the eye to detect, all winter long, but came idly out into the woods and fields with returning spring, leaping and singing, wild with affectionate joy. They were not allowed to ramble about in their own shapes; therefore, they changed themselves to doves and butterflies and winged their way to good mortals, whom they guarded from all harm.

Some Greek fairies

The Korrigans of Brittainy, mentioned earlier, were peculiar in many ways. They had beautiful singing voices and bright eyes, but they never danced. They preferred to sit still at twilight, like mermaids, combing their long golden hair. The tallest of them was nearly two feet high, fair as a lily and transparent as dew itself, yet able as the rest to seem dark, hump-backed, and terrifying. One who passed the night with them or joined in their sports was sure to die shortly, since their very breath or touch was fatal. And again, as in the case of Seigneur Nann, about whom a touching Breton ballad was made, they doomed to death any who refused to marry one of them within three days.

Of the Native American fairies we do not know much. In Mr. Schoolcraft's books of legends, there is a beautiful little Bone-dwarf, who may almost be considered a fairy. In the land of the Sioux, they tell the pretty story of Antelope and Karkapaha, and how the wee warrior-folk, thronging on the hill, clad in deerskin, and armed with feathered arrow and spear, put the daring heart of a slain enemy into the breast of the timid lover Karkapaha, and made him worthy both to win and keep his lovely maiden, and to deserve homage for his bravery from her tribe and his. Some of you will remember one thing against the Puk-Wudjies, which is an Algonquin name meaning "little vanishing folk," to wit: that they killed Hiawatha's friend, "the very strong man Kwasind," as our Longfellow called him. He had excited their envy, and they flung on his head, as he floated in his canoe, the only thing on earth that could kill him: the seed-vessel of the white pine.

The Scotch, Irish, and English overground fairies were, as a general thing, very much alike. They had the power of becoming visible or invisible, compressing or enlarging their size, and taking any shape they pleased. When an Irish Shefro was disturbed or angry and wanted to get a house or a person off her grounds, she put on the strangest appearances: she could crow, spit fire, slap a tail or a hoof about, grin like a dragon, or give a frightful, weird, lion-like roar. Of course, the object of her polite attention thought it best to oblige her. If she and her companions were anxious to enter a house, they lifted the spryest of their number to the keyhole and pushed him through. He carried a piece of string, which he fastened to the inside knob, and the other end to a chair or stool, and over this perilous bridge the whole giggling group marched in one by one. The Irish and Scotch fays were more mischievous than the English but have not fared so well, having had no memorable verses made about them. The little Scots were sometimes dwarfish wild creatures, wrapped in their plaids, or, more often, comely and yellow-haired, the ladies in green mantles, inlaid with wild-flowers and dapper little gentlemen in green trousers, fastened with bobs of silk. They carried arrows and went on tiny, spirited horses, as did the Welsh fairies, "the silver bosses of their bridles jingling in the night-breeze."[4] An old account of Scotland says that they were "clothed in green, with disheveled hair floating over their shoulders, and faces more blooming than the vermeil blush of a summer morning."[5]

---

4   Mackie, Charles, *History of the Scottish Highlands* (Arthur Hall, Virtue, & Co., 1853)

5   Buchan, Patrick, *Legends of the North: The Guidman O' Inglismill and The Fairy Bride* (Edmonston and Douglas, 1873)

Their Welsh cousins were many. A native poet once sang of them:

—*In every hollow,*
A hundred wry-mouthed elves.[6]

They were strange little beings, and had notions of what was decorous, for they combed the goats' beards every Friday night to make them decent for Sunday. They were very quarrelsome; you could hear them snarling and jabbering like jays among themselves, so that in some parts of Wales a proverb has arisen: "They can no more agree than the fairies!" The inhabitants believed that the small ones never had courage to go through the gorse, or prickly furze, which is a common shrub in that country. One sick old woman, who was bothered by the *Tylwyth Teg* ("the fair family") souring her milk and spilling her tea, used to choke up her room with the furze and make such a hedge about the bed that nothing larger than a needle could be so much as pointed at her. In Breconshire, the Tylwyth Teg gave loaves to the peasantry, which, if they were not eaten then and there in the dark, would turn in the morning into toadstools! When Welsh fairies took it into their heads to bestow food and money, very lazy people were often supported in great style without a stroke of work. And the Tylwyth Teg loved to reward patience and generosity. They played the harp continuously, and, on grand occasions, the bugle, but if a bagpipe was heard among them, that indicated a Scotch visitor from over the border.

---

6   Attributed to Dafydd ap Gwilym, "On a Misty Walk / *Ar Niwl Maith*" (c. fourteenth century)

King James I of England mentions a "King and Queene of Phairie: sic a jolie courte and traine as they had!" in his *Dæmonology*. Nothing could have exceeded the state and elegance of their ceremonious little lives. According to a sweet old play, they had houses made all of mother-of-pearl, an ivory tennis-court, a nutmeg parlor, a sapphire dairy-room, a ginger hall, chambers of agate, kitchens of crystal, the jacks of gold, and the spits of Spanish needles! They dressed in imported cobweb with a four-leaved clover, lined with a dog-tooth violet, for an overcoat, and they ate (think of eating such a pretty thing!) delicious rainbow-tart, the trout-fly's gilded wing, and "the broke heart of a nightingale / O'ercome with music."[7]

But we have never heard that Chinese or Scandinavian elves could afford such luxury.

Their English dwellings were often in the bubble-castles of sunny brooks, and the bright-jacketed hobgoblins took their pleasure sitting under toadstools or paddling about in egg-shell boats, playing jaw harps large as themselves. Beside the freehold of blossomed hillocks and dingles, they had dells of their own, and palaces, with everything lovely in them, and whatever they longed for was to be had for the wishing. They had fair gardens in clefts of the Cornish rocks, where various colored flowers, only seen by moonlight, grew; they loved to walk in these gardens, tossing a posy to some mortal passing by, but if they ever gave it away, the elves were angry with them forever after. The elves liked to fish, and the crews put out to sea in funny uniforms of green, with red caps. They travelled on a fern, a rush, a bit of a weed, or even boldly bestrode the bee and the dragonfly, and they went to

---

7   Herrick, Robert, "Oberon's Feast" in *Poetical Works* (1635) p. 119

the chase, as in the Isle of Man, on full-sized horses whenever they could get them! When it came to time of war, their armies laid to like Alexander's own, with mushroom-shield and bearded grass-blades for mighty spears, and honeysuckle trumpets braying furiously! There are traditions of battles so vehement and long that the cavalry trampled down the dews of the mountainside and sent many a peerless fellow, at every charge, to the fairy hospitals and cemeteries.

An elf-traveller

Their chief and all but universal amusement, sacred to moon-light and music, was dancing hand-in-hand; what was called a "fairy-ring" was the swirl of grasses in a field taller and deeper green than the rest, which was supposed to mark their circling path. Inside these rings it was considered very dangerous to sleep, especially after sundown. If you put your foot within them, with a companion's foot upon your own, the elfin bunch became visible to you, and you heard their tinkling laughter; if, again, you wished a charm to defy all their anger, for they hated to be overlooked by mortal eyes, you had merely to turn your coat inside out. But a house built where the wee folks had danced was made prosperous.

Hear how deftly old John Lyly, nearly four hundred years ago, put the dancing in his lines:

> *Round about, round about, in a fine ring-a,*
> *Thus we dance, thus we prance, and thus we sing-a!*
> *Trip and go, to and fro, over this green-a;*
> *All about, in and out, for our brave queen-a.*[8]

The elves, as we know, were governed generally by a queen, who bore a white wand and stood in the center while her merry retainers skipped about her. Fairy-rings were common in every Irish parish. One was celebrated from antiquity at Alnwick in Northumberland County in England; it was believed that evil would befall any who ran around it more than nine times. The children were constantly running around it, but nothing could

---

8   Lyly, John, *Maid's Metamorphosis* (1600)

tempt the bravest of them all to go one step farther. In France, as in Wales, the fairies guarded the cromlechs with care, and preferred to hold revel near them.

At these merry festivals, in the pauses of action, meat and drink were passed around. A Danish ballad tells how Svend-Fälling drained a horn presented by elf-maids, which made him as strong as twelve men, and gave him the appetite of twelve men, too—a natural but embarrassing consequence. It used to be proclaimed that anyone daring enough to rush on a fairy feast, snatch the drinking-glass, and get away with it would be lucky henceforward. The famous goblet, the Luck of Edenhall, was seized after that fashion by one of the Musgraves; whereat the Fairy People disappeared, crying aloud: "If that glass do break or fall, farewell the Luck of Edenhall!"[9]

Once upon a time, the Duke of Wharton dined at Edenhall and came very near ruining his host, and all his race; for the precious Luck slipped from his hand; but the clever butler at his elbow happily caught it in his napkin, and averted the catastrophe: so the beautiful cup and the favored family enjoy each other in security to this day.

In the song of "Sir Olaf," we are told how he fell in, while riding by night, with the whirling elves; and how, after their every plea and threat that he should stay from his to-be-wedded sweetheart at home and dance, instead, with them, he hears the refrain:

O the dance, the dance! How well the dance goes under the trees!

9   *The Gentleman's Magazine* (1791) part 2, p. 721

And through their wicked magic, after all his steadfast resistance, with the wild music and the dizzy measure whirling in his brain, there he dies.

All the carefree, unsteady, fantastic motion broke up at the morning rooster, and instantly the little bacchantes vanished. And, strangest of all, the betraying flash of the dawn showed their peach-like color, their blonde, smooth hair, and bodily agility changed, like a Dead Sea apple, and turned into ugliness and distortion! It was not the lovely vision of a minute back which hurried away on the early breeze, but a crowd of leering, sullen-eyed bugaboos, laughing fiercely to think how they had deceived a beholder.

These, then, were the Light Elves, not all lovable, loyal, or gentle as they were expected to be, but cruel to wayfarers like poor Sir Olaf, and treacherous and mocking, beautiful so long as they were good, and hideous when they had done a foul deed. It is hard to say wherein they were better than the Underground Elves, who were, despite some kindly characteristics, professional doers of evil and had not the choice or chance of being so happy and fortunate. But we record them as we find them, not without the sobering thought that here, as at every point, the fairies are a running commentary on the puzzle of our own human life.

CHAPTER FIVE

DEAR BROWNIE

Brownie, the willing drudge, the kind little housemate, was the most popular of all fairies; and it is he whom we now love and know best.

He was a sweet, unselfish fellow, but very wide awake as well, full of mischief and spirited as a young eagle when he was deprived of his rights. He belonged to a tribe of great influence and size, and each division of that tribe, inhabiting different countries, bore a different name. But the word *Brownie*, to English-speaking people, will serve as meaning those fairies who attached themselves persistently to any spot or any family, and who labored on behalf of their chosen home.

The Brownie proper belonged to the Shetland and the Western Isles, Cornwall, and the Highlands and Borderlands of Scotland. He was an indoor gentleman and varied in that from our friends the Dark and Light Elves. He took up his dwelling in the house or the barn, sometimes in a special corner, under the roof, or even in the cellar pantries, where he ate a great deal more than was good for him. In the beginning, he was supposed to have been covered with short curly brown hair, like a clipped water-spaniel, whence his name. But he changed greatly in appearance. Later accounts picture him with a homely, sunburnt little face (as if bronzed with long wind and weather), dark-coated, red-capped, and shod with noiseless slippers, which were as good as wings to his restless feet. Along with him, in Scotch houses and in English houses supplanting him, often lived the Dobie or Dobbie who was not by any means so bright and active ("O, ye stupid Dobie!" runs a common phrase), and therefore not to be confused with him.

Brownie's delight

Brownie's delight was to do domestic service. He churned, baked, brewed, mowed, threshed, swept, scrubbed, and dusted; he set things in order, saved many a step to his mistress, and took it upon himself to manage the maidservants and reform them, if necessary, by severe and original measures. Neatness and precision he dearly loved, and never forgot to drop a penny overnight in the shoe of a person deserving well of him. But lax offenders he pinched black and blue, and led them an exciting life of it. His favorite revenge, among a hundred equally ingenious, was dragging the disorderly servant out of bed. A great poet announced in Brownie's name:

'Twixt sleep and wake
I do them take,
And on the key-cold floor them throw!
If out they cry
Then forth I fly,
And loudly laugh I: "Ho, ho, ho!"[10]

Like all gnomes truly virtuous, he could be the worst varlet—the most meddlesome, troublesome, burdensome urchin to be imagined—when the whim was upon him. At such times, he gloried in undoing all his good deeds, and by way of emphasizing his former tidiness and industry, he tore curtains, smashed dishes, overturned tables, and made havoc among the kitchen-pans. All this was done in a sort of holy wrath, for be it to Brownie's credit that

---

10   Collier, John Payne, *The Mad Pranks and Merry Jests of Robin Goodfellow* (Stephen Austin & Sons, 1628)

if he were treated with courtesy, and if the servants did their own duties honestly, he was never other than his gentle, well-behaved, hard-working little self.

Brownie asked for no wages, had a scorn of "tipping" when he had been especially obliging, and could not be wheedled into accepting even so much as a word of praise. A farmer at Washington in Sussex, England, who had often been surprised in the morning at the large heaps of corn threshed for him during the night, determined at last to sit up and watch what went on. Creeping to the barn-door and peering through a chink, he saw two manikins working away with their fairy flails, and stopping an instant now and then, only to say to each other: "See how I sweat! See how I sweat!" —the very thing which befell Milton's "lubbar fiend" in "L'Allegro." The farmer, in his pleasure, cried "well done, my little men!" whereupon the startled sprites uttered a cry and whirled and whisked out of sight, never to toil again in his barn.

It is said that not long ago, there was a whole tribe of tiny, naked Kobolds (Brownie's German name) called *Heinzelmänchen,* who bound themselves for love to a tailor of Cologne, and did, moreover, all the washing, scouring, and kettle-cleaning for his wife. Whatever work there was left for them to do was straightway done, but no one ever beheld them. The tailor's prying spouse played many a ruse to get sight of them, to no avail. And they, knowing her curiosity and aggrieved at it, suddenly marched, with music playing, out of the town forever. People heard their flutes and violins only, for none saw the little exiles themselves, who got into a boat and sailed "westward, westward!" like "The Song of Hiawatha." The city's luck is thought to have gone with them.

Brownie relishes his bowl of cream

But Brownie, who would take neither money nor thanks, nor a glance of mortal eyes, and who departed in high dudgeon as soon as a reward was offered to him, could be bribed very prettily if it were done in a polite and secretive way. He was not too scrupulous to pocket whatever might be dropped on a stair or a windowsill, where he was sure to pass several times in a day, and walk off, whistling, to keep his own counsel and say nothing about it. And for goodies, mysterious goodies left in strange places by chance, he had excellent taste. Housewives, from the era of the first Brownie, never failed slyly to gladden his favorite haunt with the dish which he liked best, and which, so long as it was fresh and plentiful, he considered a satisfactory squaring-up of accounts. One of these desired treats was knuckled cakes, made of meal warm from the mill, toasted over the fire, and spread with honey. To other tidbits, also, he was partial, but, first and last, he relished his bowl of cream left on the floor overnight. Cream he drank and expected the world over, and in Devon, and in the Isle of Man, he liked a basin of water for a bath.

Fine clothes were quite to his mind; he was very vain when he had them, and it was what Pet Marjorie called "majestick pride," and no whim of anger or sensitiveness, which sent him hurrying off the moment his wardrobe was supplied by some grateful housekeeper, to eschew work forever after, and set himself up as a gentleman of leisure.[11] Many funny stories are told of his behavior under an unexpected shower of dry goods. Brownie, who, in his humble station, was so steadfast and sensible, had his poor head completely turned by the sight of a new bright-colored jacket. The gentle little Piskies or Pixies of Devonshire, who are of the Brownie race and very different from the malicious Piskies in Cornwall, were likewise great dandies and sure to decamp as soon as they obtained a fresh cap or petticoat. Indeed, they dropped violent hints on the subject. Think of a sprite-of-all-work, recorded as being too proud to accept any regular payment even in fruit or grain, standing up brazenly before his mistress, his sly eyes fixed

---

11   Fleming, Marjory, *The Story of Pet Marjorie* (H. B. Farnie, 1858)

on her, drawling out this absurd, whimpering rhyme (for Piskies scorned to talk prose!):

Little Pisky, fair and slim,
Without a rag to cover him!

With his lisp, and his funny snicker, and his winning impudence generally, don't you think he could have wheedled clothes out of a stone? Of course the lady humored him and made him a costly, trimmed suit; the ungrateful small beggar made off with it post-haste, chanting to another tune:

Pisky fine, Pisky gay!
Pisky now will run away.[12]

The moment the Brownie-folk could cut a respectable figure in fashionable garments, they turned their backs on an honest living and scurried away to astonish the belles in Fairyland.

Very much the same thing befell some German house-dwarves, who used to help a poor smith and make his kettles and pans for him. They took their milk evening by evening and went back gladly to their work, to the smith's great profit and pleasure. When he had grown rich, his thankful wife made them pretty crimson coats and caps and laid both where the wee creatures might stumble on

---

12 Wright, Elizabeth Mary, *Rustic Speech and Folk-Lore* (Oxford University Press, 1913), p. 209. Note that this tale is folkloric and circulated long before Guiney's writing and Wright's recording.

"Tunicam de diversis coloribus, et tintinnabulis plenam!"
was all that Pück demanded.

them. But when they had put the uniforms on, they shrieked "paid off, paid off!" and, quitting a task half-done, returned no more.

The Pisky was not alone in his bold request for his sordid little heart's desire. A certain Pück lived thirty years in a monastery in Mecklenburg, Germany, doing faithful drudgery from his youth up; one of the monks wrote, in his ingenious Latin, that on going away, all he asked was *"tunicam de diversis coloribus, et tintinnabulis plenam!"* You may put the goblin's vanity into English for yourselves. Brownie is known as *Shelley-coat* in parts of Scotland, from a German term meaning "bell," as he wears a bell, like the Rügen Dwarves, on his multi-colored coat.

The famous Cauld Lad of Hilton was considered a Brownie. If everything was left well-arranged in the rooms, he amused himself by night with pitching chairs and vases about, but if he found the place in an untidy state, he kindly went to work and put it in exquisite order. The Cauld Lad was, more likely—by his own confession—a ghost, not a true fairy. Romances were told of him, and he had been heard to sing this canticle, which makes you wonder whether he had ever heard of the House that Jack Built:

Wae's me, wae's me!
The acorn's not yet fallen from the tree
That's to grow the wood that's to make the cradle
That's to rock the bairn that's to grow to the man
That's to lay me![13]

---

13 "Song of the Cauld Lad of Hylton" (c. sixteenth or seventeenth century)

Wag-at-the-wa'

It was only ghosts who could be "laid," and to "lay" him meant to give him freedom and release, so that he need no longer go about in that bareboned and mournful state.

But the merriest of all the Brownies was in Southern Scotland, called *Wag-at-the-Wa'*. He teased the kitchen-maids much by sitting under their feet at the hearth, or on the iron crook which hung from the beam in the chimney which, of old, was meant to accommodate pots and kettles. He loved children, and he loved jokes; his laugh was very distinct and pleasant, but if he heard of anybody drinking anything stronger than home-brewed ale, he would cough virtuously and frown upon the company. Now Wag-at-the-Wa' had the toothache all the time, and, considering his twinges, was it not good of him to be so cheerful? He wore a great red-woolen coat and blue trousers, and sometimes a grey cloak over; he shivered even then, with one side of his poor face bundled up, till his head seemed big as a cabbage. He looked impish and wrinkled, too, and had short bent legs. But his beautiful, clever tail atoned for everything, and with it, he kept his seat on the swinging crook.

Scotch fairies called Powries and Dunters haunted lonely Border-mansions and behaved like peaceable subjects, beating flax from year to year. The Dutch *Kaboutermannekin* worked in mills as well as in houses. He was gentle and kind, but "touchy," as Brownie-people are. Though he dressed gayly in red, he was not pretty, but boasted a fine green tint on his face and hands. Little Killmoulis was a mill-haunting brother of his, who loved to lie before the fireplace in the kiln. This precious old employee was blessed with a most enormous nose and no mouth at all! But he had a great appetite for pork, however he managed to gratify it.

Boliéta, a Swiss Kobold, distinguished himself by leading cows safely through the dangerous mountain-paths, keeping them sleek and happy. His branch of the family lived as often in the trunk of a near tree as in the house itself.

In Denmark and Sweden was the *Kirkegrim,* the "church lamb," who sometimes ran along the aisles and the choir after service-time, and to the grave-digger betokened the death of a little child. But there was another Kirkegrim, a proper church-Brownie, who kept the pews neat and looked after people who misbehaved during the sermon.

As charming as any of these was the *Phynodderee,* or "the Hairy One," the Isle of Man's house-helper. He was a wild little shaggy being, supposed to be an exile from fairy society and condemned to wander about alone until doomsday. He was kind and obliging, and drove the sheep home or gathered in the hay if he saw a storm coming.

The *Klabautermann* was a ship Brownie who sat under the capstan, and in time of danger, warned the crew by running up and down the shrouds in great excitement. This eccentric Flying Dutchman had a fiery red head, and on it a steeple-like hat; his yellow breeches were tucked into heavy horseman's boots.

Hüttchen was a German Brownie who lived at court but dressed like a little peasant, with a flapping felt hat over his eyes. The *Alraun,* a sort of house-imp shorn of all his engaging diligence, was very small, his body being made of a root; he lived in a bottle. If he was thrown away, back he came, persistently as a rubber ball.

But that instinct was common to the Brownie race. The Roman Penates, *Vinculi terrei,* which brave old Reginald Scott called "domesticall gods," were Brownie's venerable and honorable ancestors.[14] We shall see presently what names their descendants bore in various countries. But the Russian Domovoi we shall not count among them, because they were ghostly, like the poor Cauld Lad, and seem to have been full-sized.

---

14   Scott, Reginald, *The Discoverie of Witchcraft* (1584)

CHAPTER SIX

OTHER HOUSE-HELPERS

I n modern Greece, the Brownie was known as the *Stœchia*. He was called *Para* in Finland; *Trasgo* or *Duende* in Spain; *Lutin*, *Gobelin*, and *Follet* in France and Normandy; *Niss-god-drange* in Norway and Denmark; *Tomte* in Sweden; *Niss* in Jutland, Denmark, and Friesland; *Bwbach* or *Pwcca* in Wales; in Ireland, *Fir-Darrig* and, sometimes, *Cluricaune; Kobold* in Germany; and in England, Brownie figured as *Boggart, Puck, Hobgoblin*, and *Robin Goodfellow*.

Often the Stœchia, a wayward little dark being, went about the house under the shape of a lizard or small snake. He was harmless; his presence was an omen of prosperity, and great care was taken that no disrespect was shown to him.

The services of the Para, who was a well-meaning rascal, were rather singular and not at all indispensable. He had a way of following the neighbor's cows to pasture, and milking them himself in a calf's fashion, until he had swallowed quart on quart, and was as full as a little hogshead. Then he went home, uncorked his thieving throat, and obligingly emptied every drop of his ill-gotten goods into his master's churn! How his feelings must have been hurt if anybody criticized the cheese and butter!

The Spanish house-goblin was a statelier person. He wore an enormous, plumed hat, and threw stones in a stolid and haughty manner at people he disliked. But occasionally the Duende had the form of a little busy friar, like the Monachiello at Naples.

The Lutin, or Gobelin, or Follet of French belief was likewise a stone-thrower. He was fond of children and horses, taking it upon himself to feed and caress his landlord's children when they were good, and to whip them when they were naughty; he rode the willing horses, combed them, and plaited their manes into knotty braids, for which, we may fear, the stable-boy never thanked him. He knew, too, how to worry and tease; certain French mothers threatened troublesome little folk with the Gobelin: "*Le gobelin vous mangera!*" This we may translate into: "The goblin will gobble you!" or, as in the whimsical lines of an American poet:

The gobble uns'll git you,
Ef
You
Don't
Watch
Out![15]

The Norwegian Nis was like a strong-shouldered child in a coat and peaky cap, who carried a pretty blue light at night. He

15   Riley, James Whitcomb, "Little Orphant Annie" (Bobbs-Merrill Company, 1885)

enjoyed hopping or skating across the farmyard under the moon's rays. Dogs were not allowed in his house. If he was first promised a gray sheep of his own, he would teach anyone to play the violin. Like many another of the Brownie race, he was a dandy and loved nothing better than fine clothes Tomte of Sweden lived in a tree near the house. He was as tall as a year-old boy, with a knowing old face beneath his cap. In harvest-time, he tugged away at one straw or one grain until he laid it in his master's barn, for his strength was not much greater than an ant's. If the farmer scorned his diligent little servant and made fun of his tiny load, all luck departed from him, and the Tomte went away in anger. He liked tobacco, played merry pranks, and doubled up comically when he laughed. But he had another laugh, scoffing and sarcastic, which he sometimes gave at the top of his voice.

Like the Devon Piskies, the Niss-Puk required water left at his disposal overnight. The Nis of Jutland was the Puk of Friesland. He also liked his porridge with butter. He lived under the roof, or in dark corners of the stable and house. He was of the Tomte's size; he wore red stockings on his stumpy little legs, a pointed red cap, and a long gray or green coat. For soft, easy slippers he had a great longing; if a pair were left out for him, he was soon heard shuffling in them over the floor. He had long arms, a big head, and big bright eyes, enough so that the people of Silt have a saying concerning an inquisitive or astonished person: "He stares like a Puk." Puk, too, played sorry tricks on the servants, and was indignant if he was ever deprived of his nightly bowl of groute [sauerkraut].

The Bwbach of Wales churned the cream and begged for his portion, like a true Brownie. He was a hairy, dark-skinned fellow with the best-natured grin in the world. But he had an unpleasant habit of whisking mortals into the air and generally doing flighty mischiefs.

An Irish Cluricaune

The unique Irish Cluricaune, who had that name in Cork, was called *Luricaune* and *Leprechaun* in other parts of the country. He differed from the Shefro in living alone, and in his odd appearance and habits. Though he was a house-spirit and did housework, his ambitions ran in the opposite direction, and in his every spare minute, when he was not smoking or drinking, you might have seen him—a miniature old man, with a cocked hat and a leather apron—sitting on a low stool, humming a fairy-tune, and perpetually cobbling at a pair of shoes no bigger than acorns.

The shoes were occasionally captured and shown. And as we have seen, Mr. Cluricaune was a fortune-hunter, and a very wide-awake, versatile goblin altogether. In his Brownie capacity, he once wreaked a hard revenge on a maid who served him shabbily. A Mr. Harris, a Quaker, had on his farm a Cluricaune named Little Wildbeam. Whenever the servants left the beer-barrel running through negligence, Little Wildbeam wedged himself into the hole and stopped the flow, at great inconvenience to his poor little body, until someone came to turn the knob. So, the master bade the cook always put a good dinner down cellar for Little Wildbeam. One Friday, she had nothing but part of a herring and some cold potatoes, which she left in place of the usual feast. That very midnight, the fat cook got pulled out of bed and thrown down the cellar-stairs, bumping from side to side, so that it made her very sore indeed; meanwhile, the smirking Cluricaune stood at the head of the steps, and sang at the luckless heap below:

Molly Jones, Molly Jones!
Potato-skin and herring-bones!
I'll knock your head against the stones,
Molly Jones![16]

---

16   Crocker, T. Crofton, *Fairy Legends and Traditions of the South of Ireland* (William Tegg, 1862) p. 80

In Japanese houses, Brownies were also familiar comers and goers. They were important and smooth-mannered small folk, and serenely dealt out rewards and punishments as they saw fit. When they were engaged in befriending commendable children, their features had, somehow, the ingenious likeness of letters signifying "good"; and if they made it their business to plague and hinder naughty idlers, who, instead of doing their errands promptly, stopped at the shops to buy goodies, their strange little faces were screwed up to mean "bad," as you see in Japanese artists' pictures.

Japanese children and Brownies

The English names for the affable Brownie-folk bring to our minds the most wayward, frolicsome elves of all fairydom. *Boggart* was the Yorkshire sprite, and the Boggart commonly disliked children, stealing their food and playthings, wherein he differed from his kindly kindred. *Hobgoblin* or Hop-goblin was so called because he hopped on one leg. Hobgoblin is the same as Rob or Bob-Goblin, a goblin whose full name seemed to be Robert. Robin Hood, the famous outlaw, dear to all of us, was thought to have been christened after Robin Hood the fairy, because he, too, was tricksy and sportive, wore a hood, and lived in the deep forest.

A little Fir-Darrig

In Ireland lived the mocking, whimsical little Fir-Darrig, Robin Goodfellow's own twin. He dressed in tight-fitting red; *Fir-Darrig* itself meant "the red man." He had big, humorous ears and the softest and most flexible voice in the world, which could mimic any sound at will. He sat by the fire and smoked a pipe, big as himself and belonging to the head of the house. He loved cleanliness, brought good luck to his abode, and, like a cat, generally preferred places to people.

Puck and Robin Goodfellow were the names best known and cherished. There is no doubt that Shakespeare, from whom we have now our prevailing idea of Puck, got the idea of him in his turn from the popular superstitions of his day. But Puck's very identity was all but forgotten, and since Shakespeare was, therefore, his poetical "creator," we will forego mention of him here and entitle Robin Goodfellow, the same "shrewd and meddling elf," with another nickname: the true Brownie of England.

He was both house-helper and mischief-maker, "the most active and extraordinary fellow of a fairy that we anywhere meet with."[17] He was said to have had a supplementary brother called Robin Badfellow, but there was no need for that, because he was Robin Badfellow in himself, united in his whimsical little character so many opposite qualities, that he may be considered the representative elf the world over. The old Saxon *Hudkin,* the *Niss* of Scandinavia, and *Knecht Ruprecht,* the Robin of Germany, are nothing but our masquerading goblin-friend on continental soil. And in the red-capped smiling *Mikumwess* among the Passamaquoddy tribe, there he is again!

---

17   Fletcher, John, *The Faithful Shepherdess* (1609)

He was known earlier than the thirteenth century by this name of Robin, and "famosed in everie olde wives' chronicle for his mad merrie prankes" two hundred years later.[18] His biography was put forth in a black-letter tract in 1628, and in a yet better-known ballad which recited his jests and was in free circulation while Queen Bess was reigning. The forgotten annalist says very heartily, alluding to his string of aliases:

> *But call him by what name you list;*
> *I have studied on my pillow,*
> *And think the name he best deserves*
> *Is Robin, the Good Fellow!*[19]

We class him rightly as a Brownie, because he skimmed milk, knew all about domestic life, and was the delight or terror of servants, as the case might be. He was fond of making a noise and clatter on the stairs, of playing harps, ringing bells, and misleading passing travellers; and despite his knavery, he came to be much beloved by his housemates. Very like him was the German Hempelman, who laughed a great deal. But the laugh of Master Robin sometimes foreboded trouble and death to people, which Hempelman's never did.

The jolly German Kobold had a laugh which filled his throat and could be heard a mile away. But he was a gnome malignant enough if he was neglected or insulted. He very seldom made

---

18 Halliwell, James Orchard, *Tarlton's News out of Purgatory* (1590)
19 Collier, John Payne, *The Mad Pranks and Merry Jests of Robin Goodfellow* (Stephen Austin & Sons, 1628)

a mine-sprite of himself, but stayed at home, Brownie-like, and "ran" the house pretty much as he saw fit. To the Dwarves he was, however, closely related, and dressed after their fashion, except that sometimes he wore a coat of as many colors as the rainbow with tinkling bells fastened to it. He objected to any chopping or spinning done on a Thursday. Change of servants, while he held his throne in the kitchen, affected him not in the least, for the maid going away recommended her successor to treat him civilly at her peril. A very remarkable Kobold was Hinzelmann, who called himself a Christian and came to the old castle of Hüdemühlen in 1584, whose history, too long to add here, is given charmingly in Mr. Thomas Keightley's *Fairy Mythology*.

A certain bearded little Kobold lived with some fishermen in a hut, and tried a trick which was quite classic, and reminds one of the Greek story of Procrustes, which all of you have met with, or will meet with, some day. Says Mr. Benjamin Thorpe: "His chief amusement, when the fishermen were lying asleep at night, was to lay them even. For this purpose he would first draw them up until their heads all lay in a straight line, but then their legs would be out of the line! And he had to go to their feet and pull them up until the tips of their toes were all in a row. This game he would continue till broad daylight."[20]

Now all Brownies, Nissen, Kobolds, and the rest were very much of a piece, and when you know the virtues and faults of one of them, you know the habits of them all. You can understand,

---

20 Thorpe, Benjamin, *Comprising the Principal Popular Traditions and Superstitions of Scandanavia, Northern Germany, and the Netherlands*, vol. III (1852)

The persistent Kobold of Köpenick

despite the slight but steady help given in household matters, that a person so variable, exacting, and high-tempered as this curious little sprite might happen sometimes to be a great bore and might inspire his master or mistress with the sighing wish to be rid of him. It was a tradition in Normandy that to shake off the Lutin or Gobelin, it was merely necessary to scatter flaxseed where he was wont to pass, for he was too neat to let it lie there, and yet tired so soon of picking it up that he left it in disgust and went away for good. There was also a sprite named Flerus who lived in a farm-house near Ostend and worked so hard, sweeping, drawing water, and turning himself into a plough-horse that he might replace the old horse who was sick (for no reward, either, save a little fresh sugared milk). Soon, his master was the wealthiest man in the neighborhood. But a giddy young servant-maid offended him at the day's end by giving him garlic in his milk, and as soon as poor Flerus tasted it, he departed from the premises forever, very wrathful and hurt.

There were few such successful instances on record. Though Brownie was ready in every land under the sun to leave home when he took fancy, or when he was puffed up with gifts of lace and velvet so that no mortal residence was gorgeous enough for him, yet he would take no hint, nor obey any command, when either pointed to a banishment.

CHAPTER SEVEN

WATER-FOLK

There were Oreads and Naiads to people the rivers and the seas of old, but they were not fairies; in later years, the beautiful, bright water-life of Greece, with its shells and dolphins, its palaces, its subaqueous music, and its happy-hearted occupants faded wholly out of memory. No one dominant race came to replace them. Merpeople, Tritons, and Sirens we meet now and then, as did Hendrik Hudson's crew, the Moruachs of Ireland, and the Morverch (sea-daughters) of Brittainy, but they, too, were grown and half-human. They were beautiful and swift, and usually sat combing their long hair with a mirror in one hand and their glossy tails tapering from the waist. The Danish Mermaid was gold-haired, cunning and treacherous; the Havmand or Merman was handsome, too, with black hair and beard, but kind and beneficent.

The Swedish pair offered presents to those on shore, or passing in boats, in hopes to sink them beneath the waves.

England and Ireland had no water-sprites which answered to the Nix and the Kelpie, only the Merrow, who was a Mermaid. She was a fair woman with white webbed fingers. She carried upon her head a little diving-cap, and when she came up to the rocks or the beach, she laid it by; if it were stolen from her, she lost the power of returning to the sea. If her cap were taken by a young man, she very often could do nothing better than to marry him and spend her time hunting for it up and down over his house. And once she had found it, she forgot all else but her desire to go home to "the kind sea-caves," and despite the calling of her neighbors, husband, and children, she flitted to the shore, plunged into the first oncoming billow, and walked the earth no longer.

Mer-folk

Tales of these spirit-brides who suddenly deserted the green earth for their dear native waters are common in Arabic and European folklore. This characteristic was also noted in the Sea-trows of the Shetland Islands, who divested themselves of a shining fish-skin and could not find the way to their ocean-beds if it were kept out of their reach. It was the Danish sailor's belief that seals laid by their skins every ninth night and took maiden's forms wherewith to sport and sleep on the reefs. For their capture when they were warm, living and human, one had only to snatch and hide away their talisman-skin.

The strange German Water-man wore a green hat, and when he opened his mouth, his teeth as well were green; he appeared to girls who passed his lake, measured out ribbon, and flung it to them. But we must search for smaller sprites than these.

The little water-fairies who devoted themselves to drawing under whomsoever encroached on their pools and brooks, were called *Nixies* in Germany, *Korrigans* (for this was part of their office) in Brittainy, *Ondins* about Magdebourg, and *Roussalkis*—the long-haired, smiling ones—among the Slavic people.

Near Ghent, the little old Nix

The engaging Nixies were very minute and mischievous, and abounded in the Shetland Isles and Cornwall, as did the Kelpies who were like tiny horses, known even in China. They could be found sporting on the margin and foreboding death by drowning to any who beheld them, or tempting passers-by to mount and plunging with their victims headlong into the deep. The Nix-lady was recognized when she came ashore by the edges of her dress or apron being perpetually wet. The dark-eyed Nix-man with his seaweed hair and his wide hat was known by his slit ears and feet, which he was very careful to conceal. Once in a while, he was observed to be half-fish. The naked Nixen were draped with moss and kelp, but when they were clothed, they seemed to be merely small people, save that the borders of their garments, dripping water, betrayed them. They did their marketing ashore, wheresoever they were, and, according to all accounts, with a sharp eye to economy. Like the land-elves, they loved to dance and sing. Nix did not favor divers, fishermen, and other intruders on his territory, and did his best to harm them. He was altogether a fierce, grudging, covetous little creature. His comelier wife was much better-natured and befriended human beings to the utmost of her power.

Near Ghent was a little old Nix who lived in the Scheldt; he cried and sighed much and did mischief to no one. It grieved him when children ran away from him, yet if they asked what troubled his conscience, he only sighed heavily and disappeared.

The modern Greeks believed in a black sprite haunting wells and springs who was fond of beckoning to strangers. If they came to him, he bestowed gifts upon them; if not, he never seemed angry, but turned patiently to wait for the next passer-by.

The work of the Nickel

There was a curious sea-creature in Norway who swam about as a thin little old man with no head. About the magical Isle of Rügen lived the Nickel. His favorite game was to astonish the fishers by hauling their boats up among the trees.

At Arles and other towns near the Spanish border in France were the Dracs, who inhabited clear pools and streams and floated along in the shape of gold rings and cups, so that women and children bathing would grasp them and be lured under.

The Chippewa water spirits, the *Nibanaba,* were winning in appearance and wicked in disposition; the Wampanoag tribe's Pukwudgies killed many great heroes of times past.

In Wales were the Gwragedd Annwn, elves who loved the stillness of lonely mountain-lakes, and who seldom ventured into the upper world. They had their own submerged towns and battlements, and from their little sunken city the fairy-bells sent out, ever and anon, muffled silver voices. The Gwragedd Annwn were not fishy-finned, nor were they ever dwellers in the sea, for in Wales were no mermaid traditions nor any tales of those who beguiled mortals "under the glassy, cool, translucent wave."[21]

The Neck and the Strömkarl of Swedish rivers were two little chaps with hardly a hair's breadth of difference. Either appeared under various shapes, as a green-hatted old man with a long beard, out of which he wrung water as he sat on the cliffs. Loitering on a summer night on the surface, like a chip of wood or a leaf, he seemed a fair child, harping with yellow ringlets falling from beneath a high red cap to his shoulders. Both fairies had a genius for music, and the Strömkarl especially had one most marvelous tune to which he put eleven variations. Now, to ten of them, anyone might dance decorously and with safety. But at the eleventh, which was the enchanted one, all the world went mad; tables, belfries, benches, houses, windmills, trees, horses, cripples, babies, ghosts, and whole towns full of sedate citizens began capering on the banks about the invisible player and kept it up in furious fashion until the last note died away.

---

21   Geoffrey of Monmouth, *Historia Regum Britanniae (c.* 1136)

The wren was hunted in certain countries on a certain day. As the legend goes, there was a malicious fairy once in the Isle of Man—very winsome to look at—who worked a sorry Kelpie-trick on the young men of the town and inveigled them into the sea, where they perished. At last, the inhabitants rose in vengeance and, suspecting her of causing their loss and sorrow, gave her chase so hard and fast by land that, to save herself, she changed her shape into that of an innocent brown wren. Because she had been so treacherous, a spell was cast upon her, inasmuch as she was obliged every New Year's Day to fly about as that same bird until she should be killed by a human hand. From sunrise to sunset, therefore, on the first bleak day of January, all the men and boys of the island fired at the poor wrens, stoned them, and entrapped them in the hope of reaching the one guilty fairy among them. As they could never be sure that they had captured the right one, they kept on year by year, chasing and persecuting the whole flock. But every dead wren's feathers they preserved carefully and believed that it hindered them from drowning and shipwreck for those twelve months, and they took the feathers with them on voyages great and small, in order that the bad fairy's magic may never be able to prevail, as it had prevailed of yore with their unhappy brothers.

There was terror in the presence of the sea-fairies, and only the strongest and most watchful could hope to be victorious against their arts. Their sport was to desolate peaceful homes and bring destruction on gallant ships. They, dwelling in streams and in the ocean the world over, were like the waters they loved: gracious and noble in aspect, and meaning danger and death to the unwary. We fear that, like the earth-fairies, they were quite heartless.

Hob in Hobhole

But it may be that the gentle Nixies had only a blind longing for human society and would not willingly have wrought harm to the creatures of another element. We are more willing to excuse their wrongdoing than the like fault in our frowzy under-ground folk, for somehow ugliness seems not so shocking when allied with evil as beauty does, which was destined for everyone's uplifting delight. As the air-elves had their Fairyland whither mortal children wandered and whence they returned after an unmeasured lapse of time, still children, to the ivy-grown ruins of their homes, so the water-elves had a reward for those they snatched from Earth. Legends assure us the wave-rocked prisoners a hundred fathoms down never grew old, but kept the flush of their last morning rosy ever on their brows.

Among a little community full of guile, there is great comfort in spotting one honest, kind water-boy, who, not content with being harmless as were the Flemish and Grecian Nixies, put himself to work to do good, and charm away some of the worries and ills that burdened the upper world. His name was Hob, and he lived in Hobhole, which was a cave scooped out by the beating tides in old Northumbria.

The lean pockets of the neighboring doctors were partly attributed to this benignant little person, for he set up an opposition, and his specialty was the cure of whooping cough. Many a Scotch mother took her child to the spray-covered mouth of the wise goblin's cave, and sang in a low voice:

Hobhole Hob!
Ma bairn's gotten t' kink-cough:
Tak't off! tak't off![22]

And so he did, sitting there with his toes in the sea. For Hobhole Hob's small sake, we can afford to part friends with the whole naughty race of water-folk.

---

22   Henderson, William, *Notes on the Folk-Lore of the Northern Counties of England and the Borders* (Pub. For the Folk-Lore Society by W. Satchell, Peyton and co., 1879) p. 264

CHAPTER EIGHT

MISCHIEF-MAKERS

The fairy-fellows who made a regular business of mischief-making seemed to have two favorite ways of setting to work. They either saddled themselves with little boys and spilled them, sooner or later, into the water, or else they danced along, holding a twinkling light, and led anyone so foolish as to follow them into chasms and quagmires. Their jokes were grim and hurtful and not merely funny like Brownies, for Brownie usually gave his victims (except in Molly Jones's case) nothing much worse than a pinch. So, people came to have great awe and horror of the heartless goblins who waylaid travelers and left them broken-limbed or dead.

Very often quarrelsome, disobedient, or vicious folk fell into the snare of a Kelpie, or a Will-o'-the-Wisp, for the little whippersnappers had a fine eye for poetical justice and dealt out punishments with the nicest discrimination. We never hear that they troubled good, steady mortals, but only that sometimes they beguiled them for sheer love into Fairyland.

We know that all "ouphes and elves" could change their shapes at will; therefore, when we spy fairy-horses, fairy-lambs, and such

77

quadrupeds, we guess at once that they are only roguish small gentlemen masquerading. Never for the innocent fun of it, either, but (alas!) to bring silly persons to grief.

The Irish Pooka was a horse too

In Hampshire, England, was a spirit known as *Coltpixy*, which, itself shaped like a miniature neighing horse, beguiled other horses into bogs and morasses. The Irish *Pooka* or *Phooka* was a horse too, and a famous rascal. He lived on land and was something like the

Welsh Gwyll: a tiny, black, wicked-faced wild colt, with chains dangling about him. Again, he frisked around in the shape of a goat or a bat. Spenser has him:

Ne let the Pouke, ne other evill spright, ...
Ne let hobgoblins, names whose sense we see not,
Fray us with things that be not.[23]

"Fray," as you are likely to guess, means to frighten or scare.

Kelpies, who were Scotch, haunted fords and ferries, especially in storms; allured bystanders into the water; or swelled the river so that it broke the roads and overwhelmed travellers.

Very much like them were the Brag, the little Shoopil-tree of the Shetland Islands, and the Nick, who was the Icelandic Nykkur-horse. All gamesome deceivers, who enticed children and others to bestride them, and who were treacherous as quicksand every time. And there were many more of the Kelpie kingdom, of whom we can hunt up no clues.

A man who saw a Kelpie gave himself up for lost, for he was sure, by hook or crook, to meet his death by drowning. Kelpie, familiar so far away as China, never stayed in the next-door countries of Ireland or England long enough to be recognized. They knew nothing of him by sight, nor of the Nix, his cousin, nor of anything resembling them. In Ireland lived the Merrow, but she was only an amiable mermaid.

---

23   Spenser, Edmund, "Epithalamion" in *The Works of Edmund Spenser* (Wills P. Hazard, 1857)

Will-o'-the-Wisp

The Japanese had a water-dragon called *Kappa,* whose office it was to swallow bad children who went to swim in disobedience to their parents' commands, and at improper times and places. In the River Tees was a green-haired lady named Peg Powler, and in some streams in Lancashire one christened Jenny Greenteeth, two hungry goblins whose only delight was to drown and devour unlucky travelers. But we know already that the water-sprites were more than likely to behave in such a way.

In Provence, there is a tale told of seven little boys who went out at night against their grandmother's wishes. A little dark pony came prancing up to them, and the youngest clambered on his sleek back, and after him the whole seven joined, one after the other, which was quite a wonderful weight for the wee creature, but his back kept growing longer and larger to accommodate them. As they galloped along, the children called to their playmates who were out of doors to join them, the obliging nag stretching and stretching until thirty pairs of young legs dangled at his sides! Then he made straight for the sea and plunged in, drowning them all.

The Piskies (or *Pigseys*) of Cornwall were naughty and unsociable. Their great trick was to entice people into marshes by making themselves look like a light held in a person's hand or a light in a friendly cottage window. Pisky also rode the farmers' colts hard and chased the farmers' cows. For all his diabolical behavior, you had to excuse him in part when you heard his hearty fearless laugh; it was so merry and sweet. "To laugh like a Pisky" passed into a proverb. The *Barguest* of Yorkshire, like the *Osschaert* of the Netherlands, was an open-air bugaboo whose presence always portended disaster. Sometimes he appeared as a horse or dog, merely to play the old trick with a false light and to vanish, laughing.

The *Tückebold* was a very malicious chap, carrying a candle, who lived in Hanover; his blood relative in Scandinavia was the *Lyktgubhe.* Over in Flanders and Brabant was one *Kludde,* a fellow whisking here and there as a half-starved little mare, cat, frog, or a bat, but who was always accompanied by two dancing blue flames and who could overtake anyone as swiftly as a snake. The *Ellydan* (*dan* is a Welsh word meaning "fire," and also a lure or a snare: a "luring elf-fire") was a rogue with wings, wide ears, a tall cap and two huge torches, who precisely resembled the English Will-o'-the-Wisp, the Scandinavian Lyktgubhe, and the Breton *Sand Yan y Tad.* Black Americans make him out Jack-o'-Lantern: a vast, hairy, goggle-eyed, big-mouthed ogre, leaping like a giant grasshopper and forcing his victims into a swamp, where they died. The gentlemen of this tribe preferred to walk abroad at night, like any other torchlight procession. Their little bodies were invisible, and the traveler who hurried towards the pleasant lamp ahead never knew that they were being tricked by a grinning fairy, until they stumbled upon the brink of a precipice or found themselves knee-deep in a bog. Then the brazen little guide shouted outright with glee, put out his mysterious flame, and somersaulted off, leaving the poor tourist to help themselves. The only way to escape his arts was to turn your coat inside out.

You may guess that the ungodly wights had plenty of fun in them, by this anecdote: a great many Scotch Jack-o'-Lanterns, as they are often called, were once bothering the horse belonging to a clergyman, who was returning home with his servant late at night. The horse reared and whinnied, and the clergyman was alarmed, for a thousand impish fires were waltzing before the wheels. Like a good man, he began to pray aloud, to no avail. But the servant just roared, "wull ye be aff noo, in the deil's name!" Sure enough, in a wink, there was not a goblin within gunshot.

Pisky also chased the farmers' cows

There were some freakish fairies in old England, whose names were *Puckerel, Hob Howland, Bygorn, Bogleboe, Rawhead,* and *Bloodybones;* the last two were certainly scarers of nurseries.

The Boggart was a little specter who haunted farms and houses, like Brownie or Nis, but he was usually a sorry busybody, tearing the bed-curtains, rattling the doors, whistling through the keyholes, snatching his bread-and-butter from the baby, playing pranks upon the servants, and doing all manner of mischief.

Red Comb was a tyrant

The Dunnie in Northumberland was fond of annoying farmers. When night came, he gave them and himself a rest and hung his long legs over the crags, whistling and banging his idle heels. Red Comb or Bloody Cap was a tyrant who lived in every Border castle, dungeon, and tower. He was short and thick-set, long-toothed and skinny-fingered, with big red eyes, grisly flowing hair, and iron boots, a pikestaff in his left hand, and a red cap on his ugly head.

The village of Hedley, near Ebchester in England, was haunted by a churlish imp known far and wide as the Hedley Gow. He took the form of a cow and amused himself at milking-time with kicking over the pails, scaring the maids, and calling the cats, of whom he was fond, to lick up the cream. Then he slipped the ropes and vanished with a great laugh. In northern Germany we find the Hedley Gow's next-of-kin, and there, too, were little underground beings who accompanied the maids to milking and drank up what was spilt, but if nothing happened to be spilt in measuring out the quarts, they got angry, overturned the pails, and ran away. These jackanapes were a foot and a half high, and dressed in black with red caps.

Many ominous fairies, such as the Banshee, portended misfortune and death. The Banshee had a high shrill voice and long hair. Once in a while, she seemed to be as tall as an ordinary woman, very thin with her head uncovered and a floating white cloak, wringing her hands and wailing. She attached herself only to certain ancient Irish families and cried under their windows when one of their kind was sick and doomed to die. But she scorned families who had a dash of Saxon or Norman ancestry and would have nothing to do with them.

Every single fairy that ever was known to the annals of this world was, at times, a mischief-maker. They could no more keep out of mischief than a trout out of water. What lives the dandiprats led; our poor great-great-great-great grandparents! As a very clever writer put it:

A man could not ride out without risking an encounter with a Puck or a Will-o'-the Wisp. He could not approach a stream in safety unless he closed his ears to the sirens' songs, and his eyes to the fair form of the mermaid. In the hillside were the dwarfs, in the forest Queen Mab and her court. Brownie ruled over him in his house, and Robin Goodfellow in his walks and wanderings. From the moment a Christian came into the world until his departure therefrom, he was at the mercy of the fairy-folk, and his devices to elude them were many. Unhappy was the mother who neglected to lay a pair of scissors or of tongs, a knife or her husband's breeches, in the cradle of her new-born infant; for if she forgot, then was she sure to receive a changeling in its place. Great was the loss of the child to whose baptism the fairies were not invited, or the bride to whose wedding the Nix, or water-spirit, was not bidden. If the inhabitants of Thale did not throw a black cock annually into the Bode, one of them was claimed as his lawful victim by the Nickelmann dwelling in that stream. The Russian peasant who failed to present the Rusalka or water-sprite he met at Whitsuntide, with a handkerchief, or a piece torn from his or her clothing, was doomed to death.[24]

One had to be ever on the lookout to escape the sharp little immortals, whose very kindness to people was a species of coquetry and who never spared their friends' feelings at the expense of their own saucy delight.

---

24   Pennell, Elizabeth Robins, "Relation of Fairies to Religion" (The Atlantic, October 1844) p. 466

CHAPTER NINE

PUCK AND POETS' FAIRIES

Puck, as we said, is Shakespeare's fairy. There is some probability that he found in *Cwm Pwca*, or "Puck Valley," a part of the romantic glens of Clydach in Breconshire, the original scenes of his fanciful *A Midsummer Night's Dream*. This glen used to be crammed with goblins. There, and in many like-named Welsh places, Puck's pranks were well-remembered by old inhabitants. This Welsh Puck was an odd little figure, long and grotesque, and looked something like a chicken half out of his shell—at least, this is how a peasant drew him from memory with a bit of coal. *Pwcca*, or *Pooka* in Wales, was but another name for Ellydan; his favorite joke was also to travel along before a wayfarer with a lantern held over his head, leading miles and miles, until he got to the brink of a precipice. Then the little wretch sprang over the chasm, shouted with wicked glee, blew out his lantern, and left the startled traveler to reach home as best they could. Old Reginald Scott must have had this sort of a Puck in mind when he put Kitt-with-the-Candlestick, whose identity troubled the critics much, in his catalogue of "bugbears."

The very old word *Pouke* meant "the devil" (horns, tail, and all). From that word, as it grew more human and serviceable, came the Pixy of Devonshire, the Irish Phooka, the Scottish Bogle, and the Boggart in Yorkshire, and even one nursery-tale title of Bugaboo. Oddest of all, the name *Pug,* which we give now to an amusing race of small dogs, is an everyday reminder of poor lost Puck and of the strange changes which, over a century or two, may befall a word. Puck was considered court-jester, a mild, comic, playful creature:

A little random elf
Born in the sport of Nature, like a weed,
For simple sweet enjoyment of myself,
But for no other purpose, worth or need;
And yet withal of a most happy breed.[25]

But he kept to the last his character of practical joker and his alliance with his grim little cousins, the Lyktgubhe and the Kludde. Glorious old Michael Drayton made a verse of his naughty tricks, which you shall hear:

This Puck seems but a dreaming dolt,
Still walking like a ragged colt,
And oft out of a bush doth bolt
On purpose to deceive us;

25   Shakespeare, William, *A Midsummer Night's Dream* (c. 1595–6)

And leading us, makes us to stray
Long winter nights out of the way:
And when we stick in mire and clay,
He doth with laughter leave us.[26]

The Welsh Puck

---

26   Colt, William, *Nymphidia* (1627)

Shakespeare, who calls him a "merry wanderer of the night" and allows him to fly "swifter than arrow from the Tartar's bow" was the first to make Puck into a house spirit.[27] The poets were especially attentive to the offices of these house spirits.

According to the poets, Mab and Puck do everything indoors, which we think is characteristic of a Brownie. William Browne, born in Tavistock, in the county of Devon, where the Pixies lived, prettily puts it how the fairy-queen did:

—command her elves
To pinch those maids that had not swept their shelves;
And further, if by maiden's oversight,
Within doors water was not brought at night,
Or if they spread no table, set no bread,
They should have nips from toe unto the head!
And for the maid who had performed each thing
She in the water-pail bade leave a ring.[28]

Herrick confirms what we have just heard:

If ye will with Mab find grace,
Set each platter in its place;
Rake the fire up, and get
Water in ere the sun be set;

27 Shakespeare, William, *A Midsummer Night's Dream* (c. 1595–6)
28 Browne, William, "Brittania's Pastorals" in *The Poems of William Browne of Tavistock* (Lawrence and Bulleh, 1894) p. 61. Originally printed in 1616.

Wash your pails, and cleanse your dairies;
Sluts are loathsome to the fairies!
Sweep your house: who doth not so,
Mab will pinch her by the toe.[29]

A merry Night-Wanderer

---

29   Herrick, Robert, "The Fairies" in *Works of Robert Herrick, vol. I* (London, Lawrence & Bullen, 1891) p. 252

"By the moon we sport and play."

John Lyly has this charming fairy song in his very beautiful play *Maid's Metamorphosis*, which takes us out to the grass, the soft night air, the softer starshine:

By the moon we sport and play;
With the night begins our day;
As we dance, the dew doth fall.
Trip it, little urchins all!
Lightly as the little bee,
Two by two, and three by three,
And about go we, and about go we.[30]

---

30   Lyly, John, *Maid's Metamorphosis* (1600)

What a picture of the wee tribe at their revels! Here is another, from Ben Jonson's *Sad Shepherd*:

Span-long elves that dance about a pool,
With each a little changeling in her arms.[31]

In Lyly's play just mentioned, Mopso, Joculo, and Prisio have something in the way of a pun for each fairy they address:

Mop.: *I pray you, what might I call you?*

First Fairy: *My name is Penny.*

Mop.: *I am sorry I cannot purse you!*[32]

Pris.: *I pray you, sir, what might I call you?*

Second Fairy: *My name is Cricket.*

Pris.: *I would I were a chimney for your sake!*

Joc.: *I pray you, you pretty little fellow, what's your name?*

Third Fairy: *My name is Little Little Prick.*

---

31   Jonson, Ben, *Sad Shepherd* (1641)

32   Mr. Keightley says that the Crickets were a family of great note in Fairyland; many poets celebrated them.

Joc.: *Little Little Prick! O you are a dangerous fairy, and fright
all the little wenches in the country out of their beds. I care not
whose hand I were in, so I were out of yours.*

Drayton gives us a list of tinkling elfin ladies' names, which
are pleasant to hear as the drip of an icicle:

*Hop and Mop and Drop so clear,
Pip and Trip and Skip that were
To Mab their sovereign ever dear,
Her special maids-of-honor:*

*Pib and Tib and Pinck and Pin,
Tick and Quick, and Jil and Jin,
Tit and Nit, and Wap and Win,
The train that wait upon her!*[33]

Young Thomas Randolph has an equally delightful account
in his pastoral drama *Amyntas*, of his wee folk orchard-robbing,
whose chorused Latin Leigh Hunt thus roguishly translates:

*We the fairies blithe and antic,
Of dimensions not gigantic,
Tho' the moonshine mostly keep us,
Oft in orchard frisk and peep us.*

---

33   Drayton, Michael, *Nymphidia* (1627)

Stolen sweets are always sweeter;
Stolen kisses much completer;
Stolen looks are nice in chapels;
Stolen, stolen, be our apples!

When to bed the world is bobbing,
Then's the time for orchard-robbing:
Yet the fruit were scarce worth peeling,
Were it not for stealing, stealing![34]

You will notice that Shakespeare places his Gothic goblins in the woods about Athens, a place where real fairies never set their rose-leaf feet, but where once sported yet lovelier Dryads and Naiads. These dainty British Greeks are very small indeed: Titania orders them to make war on the rear-mice [bats] and make coats of their leather wings. Mercutio's Queen Mab is scarce bigger than a snowflake. Prospero, in *The Tempest*, commands, besides his "delicate Ariel," all "…elves of hills, brooks, standing lakes, and groves."[35]

The make-believe fairies in *The Merry Wives* know how to pinch offenders black and blue. The shepherd, in the *Winter's Tale*, takes the baby Perdita for a changeling. All the Shakespeare people seem wise in goblin-lore.

---

34   Randolph, Thomas, *Amyntas*, trans. James Henry Leigh Hunt (T. and J. Allman, 1820)

35   Shakespeare, William, *The Tempest* (1611)

You see that we have looked for the literature of our pretty friends only among the old poets—and only English poets at that—but the foreign fairies are no less charming. Chaucer and Spenser loved the brood especially. Robert Herrick knew all about "the elves also, / Whose little eyes glow."[36]

Sir Philip Sidney smiled upon them once or twice, and great Milton could spare them a line of his majestic verse. But the high tide of their praise was ebbing already when Dryden and Pope were writing. Lesser poets than any of these, Parnell and Tickell, wrote fairy tales, but they lack the relish of the honeyed rhymes Drayton, Lyly, and supreme Shakespeare, give us. Keats was drawn to them, though he has left us but sweet and brief proof of it, and Thomas Hood, of all gentle poets, has done most for the "small foresters." In prose, the fairies are "famoused" east and west; they may sing their loudest canticle to the good Brothers Grimm in Fairyland. The arts have been their handmaids, and some of this world's most lovable spirits have delighted to do them merry honor: Mendelssohn in his quicksilver orchestral music, and dear Richard Doyle in the quaintest drawings that ever fell, laughing, from a pencil-point.

36   Herrick, Robert, "The Night Piece, to Julia" *in Hesperides; or, The Works Both Humane and Divine of Robert Herrick* (1648)

The Elves whose little eyes glow

CHAPTER TEN

CHANGELINGS

Kidnapping was a favorite pastime with our small friends, and a great many reasons concurred to make it a necessary and thriving trade. We are told that both the Tylwyth Teg and the Korrigans had a fear that their frail race was dying out and sought to steal hearty young children, leaving the wee, bright, sickly "changeling," or ex-changeling in its place. That sounds like a quibble, for we know that fairies were free from the shadow of death and could not possibly dread any lessening of their numbers from the old cause. Yet we saw that the air-elves held pitched battles and murdered one another like gallant soldiers from the world's beginning. Again comes a straggling little proof to make us suspect that they did not quite have the immortality they boasted. However, we pass it by, at least sure that the philosopher who first observed the merry goblins at the bottom, wavering and disconsolate, recognized an instance of it in this pathetic eagerness to adopt babies not their own. Fairy-folk were believed, in general, to have power over none but unbaptized children.

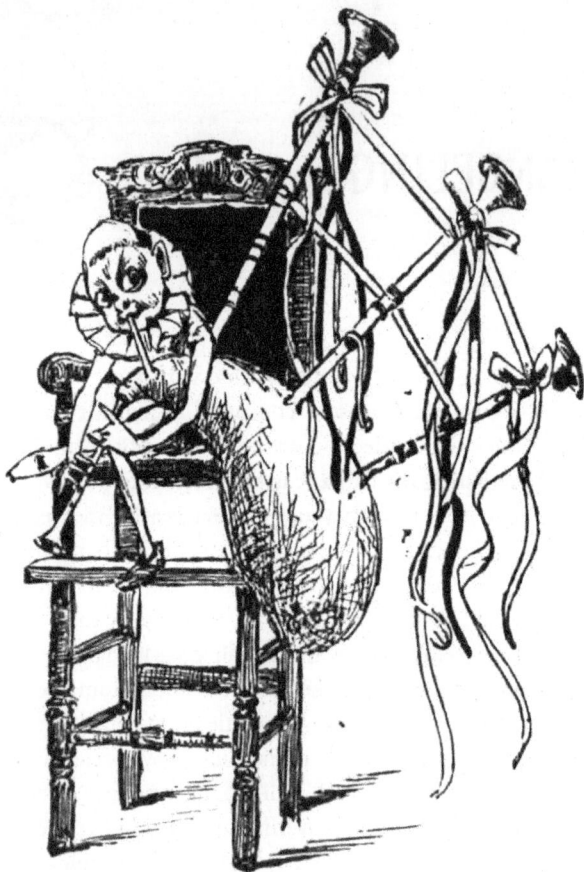

There was an Irish changeling...

A tradition older and wider than the Tylwyth Teg's states that a yearly tribute was due from Fairyland to the prince of the infernal regions, as poor King Ægeus had once to pay Minos of Crete with the seven fair children. For the sake of sparing their own dear ones, the little beings in their fantastic dress flew east and west on an anxious hunt for human children, who might be captured and delivered over to bondage instead. They crept cautiously to many a cradle and having secured the sleeping innocent, "plucked the nodding nurse by the nose," as Ben Jonson said, and vanished with a scream of triumphant laughter.[37] Welsh fairies have been caught in the very act of the theft, and a pretty fight they made every time to keep their booty, but the strength of a human, was, of course, too much for them to resist for long.

Now, whenever a mother who, you may count upon it, thought her own urchin most beautiful of all under the moon, found him growing cross and homely in despite of herself, she suddenly awoke to this view of the case: the dwindled babe was her babe no longer, but a miserable young gosling from Fairyland slipped into its place. A miserable young foreign gosling it was from that hour, though it had her own grandfather's special kind of a nose on its unmistakable face.

The discovery always been sensational: people came from the surrounding villages to wonder at the lean, gaping, knowing-eyed small stranger in the crib, and to propose all sorts of charms which should rid the house of his presence and restore the rightful heir again. They were not especially polite to the poor changeling. In Denmark and Ireland, they jiggled them on a hot shovel! If they

---

37   Jonson, Ben, "The Witches' Song" in *The Masque of Queens* (1609)

were really a changeling, the fairies, rather than see them singed, were sure to appear in a violent fluster and whisk them away, and at the same minute to drop its former owner plump into the cradle. And if it were not a changeling, how did those poor by-gone mammas know when to stop the broiling and baking?

Mr. George Waldron, who in 1726 wrote an entertaining *Description of the Isle of Man,* recorded that he once went to see a baby supposed to be a changeling. It seemed to be four or five years old, but was smaller than an infant of six months, pale, and silky-haired, and (what was unusual) with the fairest face under heaven. It was not able to walk nor to move a joint, seldom smiled, ate scarcely anything, and never spoke nor cried, but that if you called it a fairy-elf, it fixed its gaze on you as if it would look through you. If it were left alone, it was overheard laughing and frolicking, and when it was taken up after, limp as cloth, its hair was found prettily combed, and there were signs that it had been washed and dressed by its unseen playfellows.

The main way to put the family mind at rest on the matter was to make the changeling "own up"—to force them to do something which no tender mortal in socks and bibs ever was able to do, such as dance, prophesy, or manage a musical instrument. There was an Irish changeling, the youngest of five sons, who, being teased, snatched a bagpipe from a visitor and played it in the most accomplished and melting manner, sitting up in his wooden chair, his big goggle-eyes fixed on the company. And when he knew he was found out, he sprang, bagpipe and all, into the river, which leads one to suspect that he was a sort of stray Strömkarl.

The Welsh fairies had good taste and admired wholesome and handsome children. They stole such often and left the *plentyn-ne-wid* (the change-child) for substitute, who at first was exactly like the absent nursling, but soon grew ugly, shriveled, biting, wailing, cunning, and ill-tempered. In the hope of proving whether it was a fairy-waif or not, people put the little creature through hard tests so difficult that sometimes it nearly died of acquaintance with a rod, an oven, or a well.

"The acorn before the oak have I seen."

If the bereaved parent did some very astonishing thing in plain view of the wonder-chick, that would generally entrap it into betraying its secrets. A French changeling was once moved unawares to sing out that it was nine hundred years old, at least! In Wales and Brittainy (which are sister countries), the following story appears often: a mother whose infant had been spirited away, and who was much perplexed over what she took to be a changeling, was advised to cook a meal for ten farm-servants in one eggshell. When the strange little creature, burning with curiosity, asked her from his high chair what she was about, she could hardly answer, so excited was she to hear him speak. At that he cried louder: "A meal for ten, dear mother, in one egg-shell? The acorn before the oak have I seen, and the wilderness before the lawn, but never did I behold anything like that!" And so he gave damaging evidence of his age and his unlucky wisdom.

The woman replied, "you have seen altogether too much, my son, and you shall have a beating!" Thereupon she began to thrash him until he screeched, and a fairy appeared hurriedly to rescue him; in the crib lay the round, rosy, real child, who had been missing a long while.

Now the "gentry" of modern Greece had an eye also to clever children, but they almost always brought them back, laden with gifts and lovelier in person than when they were taken from home. And if they appointed a changeling in the meantime (which they were not very apt to do), it never showed its elfin nature until it was quite grown up, unlike the uncanny goblins who were all too ready from the first to give autobiographies on the slightest hint.

The Drows of the Orkney Islands fancied larger game. They used to stalk in among church congregations and carry off pious deacons and deaconesses! (So wrote one Lucas Jacobson Debes in 1670.)

In a pretty Scotch folktale, a sly fairy threatened to steal the "lad bairn" unless the mother could tell the fairy's right name. The latter was a complete stranger, and the woman was sore worried; she went to walk in the woods to ease her anxious and aching heart and to think over some means of outwitting the enemy of her boy. Presently, she heard a faint voice singing under a leaf: "Little kens the gude dame at hame. That Whuppity Stoorie is ma name!"

When the smart lady in green came to take the beautiful lad bairn, the mother quietly called her, "Whuppity Stoorie!" Off she hurried with a cry of fear, like the Austrian dwarf Kruzimügeli, the dear *Ekke Nekkepem* of Friesland, and many others who tried to play the same trick and who were always themselves the means of telling mortals the very names they would conceal.

Fairy-folk, young and old, were coquettish enough about their names and greatly preferred they should not be spoken outright. This habit got them into many a scrape. The anecdote "who hurt you? Myself!" was told in Spain, Finland, Brittainy, Japan, and a dozen other kingdoms, and seems to be as old as the Odyssey. Do you remember how, in the epic poem, Ulysses tells the Cyclops that his name is *Outis,* which means "nobody"? And how, after the eye of the wicked Polyphemus has been put out, the comrades of the big, blinded fellow ask him who did the deed, and he, very sensibly, growls back: "Nobody!" Consider what follows a typical modern version of the same trick.

"Ainsel."

A young Scotch child, whom we will call Alan, sits by the fire when a pretty creature the size of a doll waltzes down the chimney to the hearth and begins to frolic. When asked its name it says shrewdly, "Ainsel" which to the boy sounds like what it really is— "Ownself"—and makes him, when it is his turn to be questioned, as saucy and reticent as he supposes his elfin playfellow to be. So, Alan tells the sprite that his name is "My Ainsel," and gets the better of it. For bye-and-bye they wax very frisky and friendly, and right in the middle of their sport, when little Alan pokes the fire and gets a spark by chance on Ainsel's foot, he roars with pain, and the old fairy-mother appears instantly, crying angrily: "Who has hurt thee? Who has hurt thee?" The elf blurts, of course, "My Ainsel!" She kicks him unceremoniously up chimney, and bids him stop whimpering since the burn was of his own silly doing! Alan, meanwhile, climbs upstairs to bed, rejoicing to escape the vengeance of the fairy-mother and chuckling in his sleeve at the funny turn things took.

CHAPTER ELEVEN

FAIRYLAND

"And never would I tire, Janet,
In Fairyland to dwell."[38]

So runs the song. Who would weary of so sweet a place? At least, we think of it as a sweet place, but like this own world of ours, it was whatever one's eyes made it: good and gracious to the good, troublous to the evil. According to an old belief, a mean, angry, or untruthful person always exposed themselves, by the very violence of their wrongdoing, to become an inmate of Fairyland; for such a one, it could not have been all sunshine. A foot set upon the fairy-ring was enough to cause a mortal to be whisked off, pinched, bewildered, and left far from home. It was a strange experience, and it is recorded that many became loosed from earth and cloistered for uncounted years, only to return, like our Catskill hero Rip Van Winkle, after what he supposes to be a little time to find that

---

generations had passed away. Those absent took no thought of time's passing, and on reaching earth again, would begin where their lips had dropped a sentence half-spoken a hundred years before. Tales of such truants are common the world over.

Gitto Bach and the fairies

Gitto Bach (little Griffith) was a Welsh farmer's boy who looked after sheep on the mountain top. When he came home at evenfall, he often showed his brothers and sisters bits of paper stamped like money. Now when it was given to him, it was real money; but the fairy-gifts would not bear handling and turned useless and limp as soon as Gitto showed them. One day, he did not return. After two years, his mother found him one morning at the door, smiling and with a bundle under his arm. She asked him, with many tears, where he had been so long, while they had mourned for him as dead. "It is only yesterday I went away!" said Gitto. "See the pretty clothes the mountain-children gave me, for dancing with them to the music of their harps." And he opened his bundle and showed her a beautiful dress: but his mother saw it was only paper, after all, like the fairy money.

Kaguyahime, the Moon-Maid

Our pretty friends enjoyed beguiling mortals into their shining underworld with song, caresses, and winning promises. Once the mortal entered, they were met with warm welcomes from all, and the most exquisite meat and drink were set before them.

Now, if they had but the courage to refuse it, they soon found themselves back on earth, whence they were stolen. But if they yielded to temptation and their tongue tasted fairy food, they could not behold the hills of their home again for years and years. And when, after that exquisite imprisonment, they should be torn from their delights and set back at their father's door, they should find their memory almost forgotten and others sitting with a claim in their empty seat. They should not remember how long they had been missing but grow silent and depressed, and sit for hours with dreamy eyes on lonely slopes and wildwood bridges, not desiring fellowship of any soul alive, but with a heartache always for their little lost playfellows and that bright country far away, until they died.

Often, the creature who has once stood in the courts of Fairyland is placed under vow when released, and allowed to visit the earth, come back at call, and abide there always. The spell of that place is so strong no heart can escape it, nor wish to escape it. Thus ends the old romance of Thomas the Rhymer: that, at the end of seven years, he was freed from Fairyland and made wise beyond all humanity, but he was sworn to return whenever the summons should reach him. As he was making merry with his chosen comrades, a hart and a hind moved slowly along the village street. He knew the sign, laid down his glass, and smiled farewell, then followed them straightway into the strange wood, never to be seen again by mortal eyes.

A wonderful and beautiful Japanese story, too, the ancient *Taketori Monogatari*, written in the first half of the tenth century, tells us how a grey-haired bamboo-gatherer found a radiant elf-baby in a bamboo-blade, and kindly took it home to his wife; because of their great and ready generosity to the waif, the gods made them thrive in purse and health. When the little one had been with them three months, Kaguya-hime (for that was she) grew suddenly to a tall and fair girl, and so remained unchanging for twenty years while five gallant Japanese lords were doing her strange commands and running risks the world over. Though the emperor was also her suitor, and though she was unspeakably fond of her old foster-parents and grieved to go from them, she, being a moon-maid, went back in her chariot one glorious night to her shining home, whence she had been banished for some old fault, and whither the love and longing and homage of all the land pursued her.

Many sweet, wild Welsh and Cornish legends deal with shepherds and yeomen who set foot on a fairy mound by chance, or who, in some other fashion, were transplanted to the realm of the dancing, feasting elves. But they have a pathetic ending, since no wanderer ever strayed back with all his old wits sound and sharp. He seemed like one who walked in sleep and had no care or recognition for the faces that once he held dear. If he were roused too rudely from his long reverie, he died of the shock.

A merrier tale, and one which is very wise and pretty as well, is present in many literatures. The Irish version runs somewhat in this fashion, and the Spanish and Breton versions are extraordinarily like it. A little hunchback resting at nightfall in an enchanted neighborhood heard the fairies from their borderlands nearby, singing over and over the names of the days of the week. "And Sunday, and Monday, and Tuesday!" they chorused. "And Sunday and Monday and Tuesday."

The boy thought it rather hard that they do not know enough to finish their musical chant with the names of the remaining days; so, when they paused a little, very softly and tunefully he added: "And Wednesday!" The wee folk were delighted and made their chant longer by one strophe; they crowded out in their finery from the mound, bearing the stranger far down into its depths where there are the glorious open halls of Fairyland, kissing and praising their friend, and bringing him the daintiest fruit pieces ever tasted. To reward him lastingly, their soft little hands lifted the cruel hump from his back, and he ran dancing home at a year's end, to acquaint the village with his happy fortune.

The little hunchback

Now another unshapely lad, his neighbor, was racked with jealousy at the sight of his former friend made straight and fair; he rushed to the fairy-mound, and sat, scowling, waiting to hear them begin the magic song. Presently rose the silver voices: "And

Sunday, and Monday, and Tuesday, and Wednesday, and Sunday, and Monday, and Tuesday, and Wednesday." Whereat the audience broke in rudely, right in the middle of a cadence: "And Friday." The gentle elves were wrathful and swarmed out upon him, snarling and striking at him in scorn; before he escaped them, they had fastened, beside his own on his crooked back, the very hump that had belonged to the first comer! In the anecdote, as it is given by Picardy, the justice-dealing goblins are described as very small and comely, clad in violet-colored velvet, and wearing hats laden with peacock plumes. In the Japanese rendering, a wen takes the place of the hump.

Fairyland is the home of every goblin, bright or fierce, that we have ever heard of; the home, too, of the ogres, dragons, enchanted princesses, demons, and Jack-the-giant-killers of all time. The Brownies belonged there and went thither in their worldly finery when service was over; the gnomes and snarling mine-sprites; the sweet dancing elves; the fairies who stole children, romped under the river's current, or plagued honest farmers, or tiptoed it with a torch down a lonesome road—everyone there had their country and their fireside.

In that merry company were many who have escaped us and who sit in a blossomy corner by themselves, the oddest of the odd: like the Japanese *Tengus,* who have little wings and feathers like birds until they grow up, mouths very seldom opened, and most amazing big noses, with which, on earth, they were wont to fence, whitewash, write poetry, and ring bells! There, too, were the Native American wonder-babies: Weeng, whom Mr. Henry Wadsworth Longfellow in "The Song of Hiawatha" celebrates as Nepahwin, the Ojibwe god of sleep, with his numerous trains of little fairy men armed with clubs. At nightfall, he sought out mortals and, with innumerable light, blew upon their foreheads, compelling them to slumber. The great boaster, Iagoo, whom Hiawatha knew, once declared that he had seen King Weeng himself resting against a tree, with many waving and music-making wings on his back. With the Sioux and Dakota, likewise, was the spirit named Canotidan, who dwelt in many a hollow tree and the lively fellow, Taknakanx Kan. He never slept and never had time to sleep, being the god of perpetual motion. Near him, perhaps, see-sawed a couple of Chinese San Sao, or the glossy-haired Fées of Southern France pelted one another with dewdrops. There also, the African Yumboes had their magnificent tents spread: those little thieving Banshee-Brownies, wrapped in white cotton pangs, who leaned back in their seats after a gorgeous repast and beheld an army of hands appear and carry off the golden dishes! There abided, as the venerated elder of the rest, the long-bearded small men whom Homer, Aristotle, and good Herodotus had not scorned to celebrate, whom Sir John Mandeville avowed to be "right fair and gentle, after their quantities, both the men and the women…. And he that liveth eight year, men hold him right passing old…and of the men of our stature have they as great scorn and wonder as we would have among us of giants!"[39]

Of these and thousands more marvelous is Fairyland full; full of things startling and splendid and grewsome and visionary: "full of noises, / Sounds and sweet airs that give delight, and hurt not."[40]

---

39 Mandeville, John, *Mandeville's Travels* (c. 1357–1371) p. 108
40 Shakespeare, William, *The Tempest*, 1611

Any picture of it is tame, any worded description dull and heavy to you who discover it daily at first hand and who know its faces and voices, which fade too quickly from the brain. All fine adventures spring thence: all loveliest color, odor and companionship are in that stirring, sparkling world. Can you not help us back there for an hour? Who knows the path? Who can draw a map and set up a signpost? Who can bar the gate, when we are safe inside, and keep us forever and ever in our forsaken "dear, sweet land of Once-upon-a-Time?"[41]

Taknakanx Kan

---

41 Thackray Bunce, John, *Fairy Tales: Their Origin and Meaning* (MacMillan and Co., 1878)

CHAPTER TWELVE

THE PASSING OF THE FAIRY PEOPLE

There was once a very childish child who laid her fairy-book on its face across her knee and sat all the morning watching the cups of the honeysuckle, grieving that not one solitary elf was left to swing on its sun-touched edges and laugh back at her with unforgettable eyes.

We are sorry for her, and sorry with her. The Fairy People have gone away (alas!) and would that they might return! No one knows why nor when they left us, nor whither they turned their faces. The exodus was made softly and slowly, till the whole bright tribe had stolen imperceptibly into exile. Mills, steam-engines, and prowling disbelievers joined to banish them; their poetic and dreamy drama is over, their magic lamp out, and their jocund music hushed and forbidden. Or perhaps they went lingeringly and sorrowfully afar by their own accord, because the world had grown too rough for them.

"Al was this lond fulfilled of faerie."

Geoffrey Chaucer, in the fourteenth century, wrote in his sweet, tranquil fashion, which you may understand as an announcement somewhat ahead of time:

In olde dayes of the Kyng Arthour...
Al was this lond fulfilled of faerie....
I speke of mony hundrid yeer ago;
But now can no man see non elves mo.[42]

---

42 Chaucer, Geoffrey, "The Wife of Bath's Tale" in *The Canterbury Tales* (c. 1476)

For many, "elves mo" were on record after the good poet's lyre was hushed, and "thick as motes in the sunbeam" centuries after their reported flight. There have been sound-headed folk in every age, of whom Chaucer was one, who jested over the poor fairies and their arts, speaking of them only for gentle satire's sake. But though Chaucer was sure the goblins had perished, his neighbors saw manifold lively specimens of the race without stirring out of the parish. Up to two hundred years ago, prayers were said in the churches against bad fairies!

Sir Walter Scott related that the last Brownie was the Brownie of Bodsbeck, who lived there long and vanished, as is the wont of his clan, when the mistress of the house laid milk and a piece of money in his haunts. He was loath to go and moaned, "farewell to Bonnie Bodsbeck!" all night, till his departure at break of day. A girl from Norfolk, England, questioned by Mr. Thomas Keightley, admitted that she had often seen the "Frairies," dressed in white, coming up from their little cities underground. And Mr. John Brand saw a man who said he had seen one that had seen fairies!

And Mr. Robert Hunt, author of the *Drolls and Traditions of Old Cornwall,* wrote that forty years ago every rock and field in that country was peopled with them! And that "a gentleman well-known in the literary world of London very recently saw in Devonshire a troop of fairies! It was a breezy summer afternoon, and these beautiful little creatures were floating on circling zephyrs up the side of a sunlit hill, fantastically playing, 'Where oxlips and the nodding violet grow.'"[43]

---

43   Hunt, Robert, *Popular Romances of the West of England; or, The Drolls, Traditions, and Superstitions of Old Cornwall* (John Camden Hotten, 1865)

So here are three trustworthy gentlemen, makers of books on this special subject, and none of them very long dead, to offset Master Geoffrey Chaucer, and to bring the "lond fulfilled of faerie" closer than he dreamed. Around the year 1865, a correspondent told Mr. Hunt the following odd little story:

I heard last week of three fairies having been seen in Zennor very recently. A man who lived at the foot of Trendreen Hill in the valley of Treridge, I think, was cutting furze on the hill. Near the middle of the day he saw one of the small people, not more than a foot long, stretched at full length and fast asleep, on a bank of heath, surrounded by high brakes of furze. The man took off his furze-cuff and slipped the little man into it without his waking up, went down to the house, and took the little fellow out of the cuff on the hearthstone, when he awoke, and seemed quite pleased and at home, beginning to play with the children, who were well pleased also with the small body, and called him Bobby Griglans. The old people were very careful not to let Bob out of the house, nor be seen by the neighbors, as he had promised to show the man where crocks of gold were buried on the hill. A few days after he was brought, all the neighbors came with their horses, according to custom, to bring home the winter's reek of furze, which had to be brought down the hill in trusses on the backs of the horses. That Bob might be safe and out of sight, he and the children were shut up in the barn. Whilst the furze-carriers were in to dinner, the prisoners contrived to get out to have a run round the furze-reek, when they saw a little man and woman not much larger than Bob, searching into every hole and corner among the trusses that were dropped round the unfinished reek.

The little woman was wringing her hands and crying, 'O my dear and tender Skillywidden! Wherever canst thou be gone to? Shall I ever cast eyes on thee again?' 'Go 'e back!' says Bob to the children; 'my father and mother are come here too.' He then cried out: 'Here I am, mammy!' By the time the words were out of his mouth, the little man and woman, with their precious Skillywidden, were nowhere to be seen, and there has been no sight nor sign of them since. The children got a sound thrashing for letting Skillywidden escape.[44]

Fairy stories

---

44 Hunt, Robert, *Popular Romances of the West of England; or, The Drolls, Traditions, and Superstitions of Old Cornwall* (John Camden Hotten, 1865) pp. 265–6

The capture of Skillywidden

Such is the latest evidence we can find of the whereabouts of our goblins.

We may, however, consider ourselves their contemporaries, since among the peasantry of many countries, the belief is not yet extinct. But it is pretty clear to us, American as we are, that the "restless people," as the Scotch called them, are at rest and clean quit of this world. Perhaps they are satisfied, at last, of their chance of salvation, along with fortunate Christians.

Such a great system as this fairy-lore, propped on such show of earnestness grew up, not of a sudden like a mushroom after a July rain, but gradually and securely like a coral reef. The dream-building was not nonsense at all, but a way of putting what was evident and marvelous into a familiar guise. If certain strange things, which are called *phenomena,* happened—things like the coming of pebbles from clouds, music from sand, sparkling light from decay, or disease and death from the mere handling of a velvety leaf—then our forefathers, instead of gazing straight into the eyes of the fact, as we are taught to do, looked askance and made a fantastic rigmarole concerning the pebbles or the music, and passed it down as religion and law.

The simple-minded citizens of old referred any trifling occurrence, pleasant or unpleasant, to the fairies. The demons and deities, according to their notion of fitness, governed in vaster matters; the new, potent sprites took shape in the popular brain as the controllers of petty affairs. If a shepherd found one of his flock sick, it had been elf-shot; if a girl's wits went wool-gathering, it was a sign she had been in fairyland; if a cooing baby turned peevish and thin, it was a changeling! Wherever you now see a mist, a cobweb, a moving shadow on the grass; wherever you hear a cricket-chirp, or the plash of a waterfall, or the cry of the bird on the wing, there of yore were the fairy-folk in their beauty. They stood in the mind to represent the lesser secrets of Nature, to account for some wonder heard and seen. It was many a century before nations stopped romanticizing the brave things on land

and sea, and began to speculate: to observe more keenly, to hunt out reasons, and to lift the haze of their own fancy from heroic facts and deeds.

Think for a moment of the Danish moon-man, who breathed pestilence, and the moon-woman, whose harp was so charming. Well, the moon-man meant nothing else than the marsh, slimy and dangerous, which yielded a malarial odor; the wee woman with her harp represented the musical night's wind, which played over the marsh rushes and reeds. Was it not so, too, with the larger myths of Greece and Rome? For the story of Proserpine, carried away by the god of the underworld, and after a weary while, given back for half-a-year to her fond mother Ceres, tells really of the corn which is cast into the dark soil and long hidden, but reappears in glory and stays overground for months, basking in the sun. And so on with many a fable, which we read, unquestioning of the thought and purpose beneath. Though the logic was erring, we can hardly thank too much that the joyous and reverent old Paganism saw divinity in each move of Nature, kept a natural piety towards everything that lived, and made a thousand sweet memoranda to remind us forever of the wonder and charm of our earth. All mythology, and the part the fairies play in it, stands for what is true. "Still / Doth the old instinct bring back the old names" as the poet Samuel Coleridge said.[45] Again and again, when we cite some beautiful fiction of Merman and Kobold, of White Dwarf and Pooka, we but repeat (whether aware of it or not) how the dews come down at morning, or the storm-wind

---

45   Coleridge, Samuel Taylor, "Mythology" in *Parnassus: An Anthology of Poetry*, edited by Ralph Waldo Emerson (1880)

breaks the strong trees, or how a comet, trailing light, bursts headlong across the wide sky.

To comprehend fairy stories—to get under the surface of them—we would have to go over them all at great length, with exhaustless patience. And as in digging for the tendrils of a delicate, berry-laden vine, we have to search sometimes deep and wide into the woodland loam, among gnarly roots of shrubs and giant pines, in tracing the sources of the simplest tale which makes us glad or sad. We fall across a network of ponderous ancient lore, of custom, prejudice, and lost daydreams, from which this vine is hard to sever.

The spirit of these neat little goblin chronicles was right and sincere, but the matter of them was often sadly astray. Of course, sometimes useless, misleading details gathered to obscure the first idea and overrun it with a tangle of error; not only were fine stories spoiled, but many were started which were funny, or silly, or merely grim without any use beyond that.

But so powerful is truth, when there was actually a grain of it at the center, that even those versions which were exaggerated and distorted played into the hands of what we call folklore and laid their golden key at the feet of science. You will discover that, besides pointing out the workings of the natural world, the fairy tales rested often on the workings of our own minds and consciences. The Brownie was a little schoolmaster set up to teach love of order and the need of perfect courtesy; the Nix betokened anything sweet and beguiling which yet was hurtful, and to which it was—and is—a gallant heart's duty not to yield. Thus, from beginning to end, the elves at whom we laugh help us toward larger knowledge and a more chivalrous code of behavior. How shall we say, then, that there never was a fairy?

A miner, hearing the drip of subterranean water, took it to be a Duergar or a Bucca, swinging his tiny hammer over the shining ore. His notion of the Bucca, askew as it was, was one at bottom with our knowledge of the dark brooklet. You, the young heirs of mighty science, can often outstrip the slow-gathered wisdom of dead philosophers. But do not despise that fine old imagination, which felt its way almost to the light. A sixteenth-century boy, who was excited once over the pranks of Robin Goodfellow, knew many precious things which our very great nineteenth-century acuteness has made us lose!

Good-bye, then, to the army of vanishing "gentry," to their steadfast friends, and to you, dear children, who are the guardians of their wild unwritten records. Shall you not miss them when next the moon is high on the blossoming hillocks, and the thistledown, ready-saddled, plunges to be off and away? Merry fellows they were, shrewd and just; we were very fond of them, and now they are gone. Their going, like a harmony mounting note by note, ending in one noble chord and then a hush, leads us to a serious parting word. Keep the fairies in kindly memory; do not lose your interest in them. They and their history have an enchanting value, which need never be outgrown nor set aside. To the gravest mind, they bring much which is beautiful, humane and suggestive.

We have found that believers in the Fairy People were not so wrong, after all; the eye claiming to have seen a fairy saw, verily, a sight quite as astonishing. Let us think as gently of other myths to which humanity has given zeal, awe, and admiration in every faith hereafter which seems to us odd and mistaken. Many things which are not true in the exact sense are yet dear to truth and follow her as a baby's tripping tongue lisps the language of its mother, not very successfully, but still with loyalty and a meaning which attentive ears can always catch.

Surely, our ancestors loved the "span-long elves" who wrought them no great harm and gave them help and cheer. We will praise them, too. Who knows but some little goblin's thorny finger directed many an innocent human heart to march, albeit waveringly, towards the ample light of God?

GOOD-BYE

SELECT BIBLIOGRAPHY

Aytoun, William Edmonstoune. *The Ballads of Scotland, vol. II.* 1858.

Browne, William. *The Poems of William Browne of Tavistock.* Lawrence and Bulleh, 1894. Originally printed in 1616.

Buchan, Patrick. *Legends of the North: The Guidman O' Inglismill and The Fairy Bride.* Edmonston and Douglas, 1873.

Bunce, John Thackray. *Fairy Tales: Their Origin and Meaning.* MacMillan and Co., 1878.

Chaucer, Geoffrey. *The Canterbury Tales.* c. 1476.

Coleridge, Samuel Taylor. "Mythology" in *Parnassus: An Anthology of Poetry.* Edited by Ralph Waldo Emerson, 1880.

Collier, John Payne. *The Mad Merry Prankes of Robbin Good-Fellow.* Stephen Austin & Sons, 1872.

Colt, William. *Nymphidia.* 1627.

Crocker, T. Crofton. *Fairy Legends and Traditions of the South of Ireland.* William Tegg, 1862.

Dafydd ap Gwilym (attributed). "On a Misty Walk / Ar Niwl Maith." c. 1340.

Fleming, Marjory. *The Story of Pet Marjorie.* H. B. Farnie, 1858.

Fletcher, John. *The Faithful Shepherdess.* 1609.

Geoffrey of Monmouth. *Historia Regum Britanniae.* c. 1136.

Goldsmith, Oliver. *She Stoops to Conquer.* 1773.

Gomme, George Laurence, ed. *The Gentleman's Magazine Library: Being Classified Collection of the Chief Contents of the Gentleman's Magazine from 1731 to 1868: Popular Superstititions.* Elliot Stock, 1884.

Halliwell, James Orchard. *Tarlton's News out of Purgatory.* 1590.

Henderson, William. *Notes on the Folk-Lore of the Northern Counties of England and the Borders.* Published for the Folk-Lore Society by W. Satchell, Peyton, and Co., 1879.

Herrick, Robert. *Hesperides; or, The Works Both Humane and Divine of Robert Herrick.* 1648.

—. *Poetical Works.* 1635.

—. *Works of Robert Herrick, vol. I.* Reprinted by London, Lawrence & Bullen, 1891.

Hunt, Robert. *Popular Romances of the West of England or, The Drolls, Traditions, and Superstitions of Old Cornwall.* John Camden Hotten, 1865.

Jonson, Ben. "The Witches' Song" in *The Masque of Queens.* 1609.

—. *Sad Shepherd.* 1641.

James I, King of England. *Daemonologie.* 1597.

Keightley, Thomas. *The Fairy Mythology.* 1828.

Lyly, John. *Maid's Metamorphosis.* 1600.

Mackie, Charles. *History of the Scottish Highlands.* Arthur Hall, Virtue & Co., 1853.

Mandeville, John. *Mandeville's Travels.* c. 1357–1371.

Milton, John. "L'Allegro" in *Poems.* Humphrey Moseley, 1645.

Pennell, Elizabeth Robins. "Relation of Fairies to Religion." *The Atlantic,* October 1844, pp. 457–467.

Poe, Edgar Allen. "Sonnet—To Science" in *Al Aaraaf, Tamerlane, and Minor Poems.* Hatch and Dunning, 1829.

Randolph, Thomas. *Amyntas.* Translated by James Henry Leigh Hunt. T. and J. Allman, 1820.

Riley, James Whitcomb. "Little Orphant Annie." Bobbs-Merrill Company, 1885.

Scott, Reginald. *The Discoverie of Witchcraft.* 1584.

Scott, Walter. "Notes on Canto Fourth" in *Lady of the Lake.* 1810.

Shakespeare, William. *A Midsummer Night's Dream.* c. 1596.

—. *The Tempest.* c. 1611.

Spenser, Edmund. *The Works of Edmund Spenser.* Wills P. Hazard, 1857.

—. *The Faerie Queene.* William Ponfonbie, 1596.

Thorpe, Benjamin. *Comprising the Principal Popular Traditions and Superstitions of Scandanavia, Northern Germany, and the Netherlands,* vol. III. 1852.

Waldron, George. *Description of the Isle of Man.* 1726.

Wright, Elizabeth Mary. *Rustic Speech and Folk-Lore.* Oxford University Press, 1913.